VERSANT TEST PRACTICE EXAMS FOR THE 4-SKILLS PROFESSIONAL ENGLISH SCREENING, STUDENT PLACEMENT, AND WRITING TESTS WITH ANSWERS AND FREE MP3S

Versant Test Practice Exams for the 4-Skills Professional English Screening, Student Placement, and Writing Tests with Answers and Free mp3s

ISBN: 978-1-949282-83-2

Note: The Versant Test, Versant 4-Skills Test, Versant Writing Test, and Versant Student Placement Test are registered trademarks of Pearson, Inc, which is neither affiliated with nor endorses this publication.

TABLE OF CONTENTS

How to Use This Book:

The practice exams in this book are based on the skills and levels of questions on the official Versant 4-Skills Test, Versant Writing Test, and Versant Student Placement Test.

On the real Versant 4-Skills Test, you will have approximately 30 minutes to complete the exam. The test will be taken via video, and you will be able to click "Next" to go to each subsequent question.

For practice purposes, you should use this book along with the free mp3 files that accompany it.

The prompts on the audio will guide you from one question to the other.

If you are taking the Versant Writing Test for a job with Amazon, Deloitte, or another multi-national corporation (MNC), additional exercises for these exams are included beginning on page 31 of this publication. The writing test also has sentence completion, dictation, and passage reconstruction sections, so pay careful attention to those sections. You may also listen to the other sections on the audio to practice and improve your English language skills.

For those taking the Versant Student Placement Test, you should complete all of the practice questions in the 4-Skills Tests, the typing practice in the writing test section, and the read aloud and summary & opinion practice questions beginning on page 47 of the book.

We recommend taking each practice exam at least two times: the first time, as a practice test by using the book and sticking to the time limits on the prompts on the mp3.

Then listen a second time, playing the audio while looking at the answer key for each practice test, as a vocabulary and concept review.

Please see appendix 1 on page 53 for information on how to access the free mp3s for this book.

Versant 4-Skills Practice Test 1

FOR INFORMATION ON HOW TO ACCESS THE SOUND FILES, PLEASE SEE APPENDIX 1.

Part A – Repeat

Instructions: You will hear sixteen sentences or questions. Repeat each one word-for-word in the time allowed on the recording.

Example: You need to leave on the next bus.

Part B – Sentence Builds

Instructions: You will hear three groups of words in an incorrect order. After you hear them, say the sentence or question with the words in the correct order. You will hear a beep on your recording when your time for each one is finished.

Example: was looking at / my father / his favorite book

Part C – Conversations

Instructions: You will hear conversations between two people, followed by questions. Give a short simple response to each question. When you have finished all the exercises, listen to the recording again and check your answers, using the answer key at the end of the book.

Example: Speaker 1 – Maria, can you work late tomorrow?
Speaker 2 – Sure, until when?
Speaker 1 – Until 8:00 o'clock.
Question: What does Maria have to do tomorrow?

Part D – Sentence Completion

Instructions: Now refer to your test book. Please write one word that best fits the meaning of each sentence. On the real test, you will see the sentences on the computer screen and type in your response. The beeps on the recording indicate the time allowed for each one. You should play the recording as you write your answers.

Example: Should I turn right or _____ at the next corner?   *Answer:* left

1

1. You're driving too _____ . We're going to be late.

2. I need to pick up some medicine at the _____ .

3. I went to the supermarket yesterday to _____ some food.

4. The woman _____ her eyeglasses and had to buy a new pair.

5. For more _____ about the job, please see the advertisement online.

6. The return _____ needs to be provided on that letter.

7. We need to touch _____ , so give me a call tomorrow.

8. Even though she failed her last driving test, she had high _____ that she would pass this time.

9. I _____ up early this morning, so I had breakfast early.

10. You need to make an _____ if you would like to speak to the Director.

11. He was assistant manager, but now he has been _____ to manager.

12. They _____ a mistake in how they spelled my name.

13. Although you don't _____ with his methods, we still have to follow his instructions.

14. You need to use that _____ to unlock the door.

15. The college _____ a wide range of classes for the young and old alike.

16. The company caused the pollution, so they need to _____ the cost of the clean-up themselves.

17. Employees will lose pay accordingly if they are _____ to work.

18. I can finally relax now that the big project has reached an _____ .

Part E – Dictation

Instructions: Now open the word processor program on your computer. You will hear 14 sentences. Type each sentence on your computer exactly as you hear it in the time provided on the recording.

Part F – Passage Reconstruction

Instructions: For this part of the test, you will see two paragraphs. You will have 30 seconds to read each one. After 30 seconds, the paragraph will disappear from your screen. You then need to re-write the passage, using your own words in the time allowed on the recording. For this practice test, you should leave your test book open to Part F of the test and type your answer into a word processing program. You will be allowed 90 seconds to rewrite each of the passages. Please listen to the recording for the timings of the reading and the writing sections.

DO NOT LOOK AT THE PARAGRAPHS AS YOU RE-WRITE THEM!

Paragraph1:

After working for 40 years as a manager in a technology company, Paul decided to retire. Things went fine at first, and he enjoyed getting up late, spending time with his wife, and playing extra rounds of golf. However, after a few months he got bored and told his wife he was looking for something to do a couple of days a week. He signed up as a volunteer at the Red Cross and is really enjoying it.

Paragraph 2:

Matt was trying to organize a farewell party for Liz. He secretly informed all of the other co-workers about his plan. The head of the department sent a fake email to Liz, telling her to come to the conference room for her exit interview. On the appointed day, all of the co-workers assembled in the conference room, where there were gifts and refreshments. Liz then walked in to the conference room expecting her interview, but instead everyone suddenly appeared for the party.

Versant 4-Skills Practice Test 2

Part A – Repeat

Instructions: You will hear sixteen sentences or questions. Repeat each one word for word in the time allowed on the recording.

Part B – Sentence Builds

Instructions: You will hear three groups of words in an incorrect order. After you hear them, say the sentence or question with the words in the correct order. You will hear a beep on your recording when your time for each one is finished.

Part C – Conversations

Instructions: You will hear conversations between two people, followed by questions. Give a short simple response to each question. When you have finished all the exercises, listen to the recording again and check your answers, using the answer key at the end of the book.

Part D – Sentence Completion

Instructions: Now refer to your test book. Please write one word that best fits the meaning of each sentence. On the real test, you will see the sentences on the computer screen and type in your response. The beeps on the recording indicate the time allowed for each one. You should play the recording as you write your answers.

1. It is so bright and clear today. There isn't a _____ in the sky.

2. I highly _____ her for the job because she is intelligent and attentive.

3. To _____ Dan's birthday, his friends are going to have a party.

4. She was _____ from the New York branch to the Los Angeles branch.

5. Is this dress available in a smaller _____ ? This one is too big.

6. Will you please turn the lights _____ ? I want to go to sleep.

7. He arrived at the airport late, and _____ his flight, so he had to travel the next day.

8. To avoid the danger from high winds, everyone was told to leave town _____ the hurricane arrived.

9. I went on a _____ of London on a double-decker bus to go sightseeing.

10. Because of the sale, the bookstore didn't have any more televisions in _____, but they will get another delivery tomorrow.

11. To get the new product, you can _____ your order online or over the telephone.

12. I'm sorry to inform you of this at such short _____, but everyone is going to need to work late tonight.

13. Their wedding photographer was an _____, not a professional. All of their photographs turned out badly.

14. There has been peace _____ the two nations since they signed the international treaty.

15. We thought she would be _____ about going abroad, but she seemed completely bored.

16. The company was having cash flow problems and had to take out a _____ from the bank.

17. The next _____ of that product is arriving into port next week.

18. He is suffering _____ a strange illness and has been in the hospital for three weeks.

Part E – Dictation

Instructions: Now open the word processor program on your computer. You will hear 14 sentences. Type each sentence on your computer exactly as you hear it in the time provided on the recording.

Part F – Passage Reconstruction

Instructions: For this part of the test, you will see two paragraphs. You will have 30 seconds to read each one. After 30 seconds, the paragraph will disappear from your screen. You then need to re-write the passage, using your own words in the time allowed on the recording. For this practice test, you should leave your test book open to Part F of the test and type your answer into a word processing program. You will be allowed 90 seconds to rewrite each of the passages. Please listen to the recording for the timings of the reading and the writing sections.

DO NOT LOOK AT THE PARAGRAPHS AS YOU RE-WRITE THEM!

Paragraph1:

All employees are reminded to schedule their vacation days well in advance for time off this summer. Most employees want to take time off during this time off year, so the schedule may be tight in some instances. Please fill out the appropriate form. Then you will need to get approval by having your supervisor sign it. This policy will apply for any vacation days that you want to take during June, July, or August. This will help us to avoid scheduling conflicts.

Paragraph 2:

Shanika purchased a video doorbell from the store and was excited about getting home and installing it. However, when she got home, she couldn't get the doorbell to work. She returned to the store the same day to complain and get a replacement. When the sales assistant looked at the doorbell, she told Shanika that it wasn't working because she had forgotten to install batteries. Shanika felt really embarrassed about her mistake.

Versant 4-Skills Practice Test 3

Part A – Repeat

Instructions: You will hear sixteen sentences or questions. Repeat each one word for word in the time allowed on the recording.

Part B – Sentence Builds

Instructions: You will hear three groups of words in an incorrect order. After you hear them, say the sentence or question with the words in the correct order. You will hear a beep on your recording when your time for each one is finished.

Part C – Conversations

Instructions: You will hear conversations between two people, followed by questions. Give a short simple response to each question. When you have finished all the exercises, listen to the recording again and check your answers, using the answer key at the end of the book.

Part D – Sentence Completion

Instructions: Now refer to your test book. Please write one word that best fits the meaning of each sentence. On the real test, you will see the sentences on the computer screen and type in your response. The beeps on the recording indicate the time allowed for each one. You should play the recording as you write your answers.

1. Our manager told us that we will need to work harder than ever to _____ our target this month.

2. I need to _____ our reservation at the restaurant since we'll be getting there an hour later.

3. The teacher divided the work for the class project _____ all the students.

4. The workshop was very boring. I really didn't _____ it at all.

5. I _____ very deeply at night, and I have extremely vivid dreams.

6. It looks like it's going to _____, so I'd better take an umbrella.

7. Research shows that the viewing _____ of television owners have changed recently.

8. What is today's _____ ? I don't have a calendar.

9. I haven't had anything to drink since this morning, so I'm really _____.

10. Driving on that road isn't free. You need to pay a _____ at the booth.

11. It _____ to be seen whether his company will be a success or not.

12. He is wondering when the update on the project will be _____ .

13. The IT company is designing a special computer _____ for some new

    clients.

14. He mentioned that he is going to need some _____ to get the job done on

    time.

15. I'll _____ you an email to let you know how it's going.

16. The prisoner _____ from jail, but was caught two days later.

17. He was born in India, but his family _____ to the United States when he
    was a little boy.

18. She's really talented and can _____ some beautiful music on the piano.

Part E – Dictation

Instructions: Now open the word processor program on your computer. You will hear 14 sentences. Type each sentence on your computer exactly as you hear it in the time provided on the recording.

Part F – Passage Reconstruction

Instructions: For this part of the test, you will see two paragraphs. You will have 30 seconds to read each one. After 30 seconds, the paragraph will disappear from your screen. You then need to re-write the passage, using your own words in the time allowed on the recording. For this practice test, you should leave your test book open to Part F of the test and type your answer into a word processing program. You will be allowed 90 seconds to rewrite each of the passages. Please listen to the recording for the timings of the reading and the writing sections.

DO NOT LOOK AT THE PARAGRAPHS AS YOU RE-WRITE THEM!

Paragraph 1:

Marta had to call a plumber into her house to repair a pipe that was leaking under the sink. After she had paid the plumber, he left the house. She then noticed that the pipe was still leaking, so she called the plumber and asked him to return. He said that there was no need to return because he had done his job. Because of the plumber's unprofessional behavior, Marta reported him to the mayor of the city.

Paragraph 2:

Alice was riding her bicycle in the city park. It was a beautiful summer day, with the sun out and the birds singing. Alice was on the bike path and was really enjoying her day, but then suddenly she heard a strange noise, and the bike began to move in a strange way. She got off the bike and realized that the back tire was flat. She couldn't ride it in that condition, so she had to walk all the way home with her bike.

Versant 4-Skills Practice Test 4

Part A – Repeat

Instructions: You will hear sixteen sentences or questions. Repeat each one word for word in the time allowed on the recording.

Part B – Sentence Builds

Instructions: You will hear three groups of words in an incorrect order. After you hear them, say the sentence or question with the words in the correct order. You will hear a beep on your recording when your time for each one is finished.

Part C – Conversations

Instructions: You will hear conversations between two people, followed by questions. Give a short simple response to each question. When you have finished all the exercises, listen to the recording again and check your answers, using the answer key at the end of the book.

Part D – Sentence Completion

Instructions: Now refer to your test book. Please write one word that best fits the meaning of each sentence. On the real test, you will see the sentences on the computer screen and type in your response. The beeps on the recording indicate the time allowed for each one. You should play the recording as you write your answers.

1. What do you _____ for a living?

2. How much does this book _____? There's no price on it.

3. My _____ is very large. There are my parents and twelve siblings.

4. She can _____ five different languages fluently.

5. There were many guests at the celebration, so it was a bit _____ inside.

6. An increasing _____ of families are experiencing financial problems.

7. I don't _____ what he wrote to me. I'm going to tear up that letter and throw it away.

8. The game had to be _____ indefinitely because of the damage to the stadium.

9. He asked the politician a bunch of questions that she didn't have time to _____ .

10. My boss complimented me yesterday by _____ how efficient I am.

11. He was really feeling depressed. The bad news really got him _____ .

12. The supermarket has many different _____ of fruit and vegetables.

13. Littering is _____ the law, and if you do so, you will have to pay a fine.

14. You can't smoke in here. In fact, smoking is _____ in the entire building.

15. He seemed very rude. He didn't _____ "hello" or greet us in any way.

16. My parents have _____ me a great deal of support throughout my life.

17. You shouldn't swim too _____ out in the sea because of the dangerous tides.

18. She had to hurry to work today to avoid _____ late.

Part E – Dictation

Instructions: Now open the word processor program on your computer. You will hear 14 sentences. Type each sentence on your computer exactly as you hear it in the time provided on the recording.

Part F – Passage Reconstruction

Instructions: For this part of the test, you will see two paragraphs. You will have 30 seconds to read each one. After 30 seconds, the paragraph will disappear from your screen. You then need to re-write the passage, using your own words in the time allowed on the recording. For this practice test, you should leave your test book open to Part F of the test and type your answer into a word processing program. You will be allowed 90 seconds to rewrite each of the passages. Please listen to the recording for the timings of the reading and the writing sections.

DO NOT LOOK AT THE PARAGRAPHS AS YOU RE-WRITE THEM!

Paragraph 1:

Mark your calendar for the company picnic on Saturday June 11th. This year we are going to have a barbeque and live music from a band called Infinity. Please bring your spouse and children, or any other guests that you'd like to attend. The event will be held from 11:00 AM to 4:00 PM on Saturday June 11th. See you there.

Paragraph 2:

The company wants to advise everyone that we will no longer be able to offer free gym membership to our employees. Unfortunately, the gym that the company partners with has decided to double their fees because of their increased operating costs. However, if any employee would like to continue their gym membership, they may do so at half the price of the new fees. Please contact Brooke in HR for more information.

Versant 4-Skills Practice Test 5

Part A – Repeat

Instructions: You will hear sixteen sentences or questions. Repeat each one word for word in the time allowed on the recording.

Part B – Sentence Builds

Instructions: You will hear three groups of words in an incorrect order. After you hear them, say the sentence or question with the words in the correct order. You will hear a beep on your recording when your time for each one is finished.

Part C – Conversations

Instructions: You will hear conversations between two people, followed by questions. Give a short simple response to each question. When you have finished all the exercises, listen to the recording again and check your answers, using the answer key at the end of the book.

Part D – Sentence Completion

Instructions: Now refer to your test book. Please write one word that best fits the meaning of each sentence. On the real test, you will see the sentences on the computer screen and type in your response. The beeps on the recording indicate the time allowed for each one. You should play the recording as you write your answers.

1. I woke up late but arrived on _____ at the conference.

2. You will need to show your passport or some other form of _____.

3. The tasks were _____ among all the team members.

4. The building had only been finished for a month when the _____ sold it.

5. Plastic bottles can be _____ and used to make things like clothing and packaging.

6. Customers will receive a 5% _____ for ordering and paying online.

13

7. The movie star made an _____ at the film premiere.

8. He was trying to get on the boss's _____ side by giving her compliments.

9. I'm having second _____ about my plan and regret agreeing to do it.

10. Please get in touch _____ me next week so we can talk.

11. We have _____ preparing the meal, so please sit at the table.

12. I apologize. I meant to _____ you about the party last week.

13. I'm really tired of _____ to him complain all the time.

14. The movie wasn't _____. I left half-way through.

15. The company is split into two departments. The security department is _____ new, but the computing department is much older.

16. If you would like to know what my daughter looks like, have a _____ at these pictures.

17. His brother, _____ name is Samuel, is studying to become a lawyer.

18. She was fired for cheating _____ her pre-employment test.

Part E – Dictation

Instructions: Now open the word processor program on your computer. You will hear 14 sentences. Type each sentence on your computer exactly as you hear it in the time provided on the recording.

Part F – Passage Reconstruction

Instructions: For this part of the test, you will see two paragraphs. You will have 30 seconds to read each one. After 30 seconds, the paragraph will disappear from your screen. You then need to re-write the passage, using your own words in the time allowed on the recording. For this practice test, you should leave your test book open to Part F of the test and type your answer into a word processing program. You will be allowed 90 seconds to rewrite each of the passages. Please listen to the recording for the timings of the reading and the writing sections.

DO NOT LOOK AT THE PARAGRAPHS AS YOU RE-WRITE THEM!

Paragraph 1:

Neal works in a busy call center, dealing with incoming customer service calls. One day, an angry customer called and told him that the computer he bought wasn't working. The customer said the computer wouldn't even turn on. Neal informed the customer that the computer could be repaired or that the customer could receive a full refund. The customer accepted the refund, and the call ended well.

Paragraph 2:

Debbie and Karl were really excited about seeing their nephew for the first time. They bought him a little shirt with trucks printed on it, and a little toy dinosaur to play with. When they gave their nephew the present, he was so excited. He put on the new shirt right away and played with his new toy all day.

Versant 4-Skills Practice Test 6

Part A – Repeat

Instructions: You will hear sixteen sentences or questions. Repeat each one word for word in the time allowed on the recording.

_____

Part B – Sentence Builds

Instructions: You will hear three groups of words in an incorrect order. After you hear them, say the sentence or question with the words in the correct order. You will hear a beep on your recording when your time for each one is finished.

_____

Part C – Conversations

Instructions: You will hear conversations between two people, followed by questions. Give a short simple response to each question. When you have finished all the exercises, listen to the recording again and check your answers, using the answer key at the end of the book.

_____

Part D – Sentence Completion

Instructions: Now refer to your test book. Please write one word that best fits the meaning of each sentence. On the real test, you will see the sentences on the computer screen and type in your response. The beeps on the recording indicate the time allowed for each one. You should play the recording as you write your answers.

1. It was really _____ outside and no one wanted to leave the warm house.

2. I don't have my phone. I must have _____ it at the restaurant.

3. It looks like this final _____ of the letter is ready to go out.

4. Remember to _____ for her phone number when meet her.

5. I lost my _____ because I was shouting at the game yesterday.

6. I was given office supplies, consisting _____ paper and pens.

7. She said she had _____ to do with the missing money.

8. If you don't know the _____ to the question, just guess.

9. Some people like the opera, but I can't _____ it.

10. I don't like getting coffee in the mall, so I'd _____ go to that cafe in town.

11. He was speaking so softly that we couldn't _____ what he was saying.

12. I am enjoying my new job now that I have gotten used _____ it.

13. He gets the _____ grades of all the students in his class.

14. In _____ to jogging, Susan also likes to ride her bike.

15. The weather report said that people should _____ for bad weather.

16. Sarah _____ everyone my secret, but I forgave her.

17. He would have bought that new car if he'd had more _____.

18. She finally decided to _____ college after she got a scholarship.

Part E – Dictation

Instructions: Now open the word processor program on your computer. You will hear 14 sentences. Type each sentence on your computer exactly as you hear it in the time provided on the recording.

Part F – Passage Reconstruction

Instructions: For this part of the test, you will see two paragraphs. You will have 30 seconds to read each one. After 30 seconds, the paragraph will disappear from your screen. You then need to re-write the passage, using your own words in the time allowed on the recording. For this practice test, you should leave your test book open to Part F of the test and type your answer into a word processing program. You will be allowed 90 seconds to rewrite each of the passages. Please listen to the recording for the timings of the reading and the writing sections.

DO NOT LOOK AT THE PARAGRAPHS AS YOU RE-WRITE THEM!

Paragraph 1:

Thanks to all of the employees who participated in our weekend educational workshop on online security. Since the course covered password security, using networks, and avoiding spam, each employee who attended will receive a certificate indicating their attendance at these classes.

Paragraph 2:

Kay and Mark were planning on celebrating their 25th wedding anniversary on the weekend. They had arranged to stay at a hotel and eat a nice meal in a restaurant. They got in the car, and traveled into the city for their romantic evening. When they arrived at the hotel, the manager told them that they didn't have a reservation, so they decided to stay in a much more expensive hotel.

Versant 4-Skills Practice Test 7

Part A – Repeat

Instructions: You will hear sixteen sentences or questions. Repeat each one word for word in the time allowed on the recording.

Part B – Sentence Builds

Instructions: You will hear three groups of words in an incorrect order. After you hear them, say the sentence or question with the words in the correct order. You will hear a beep on your recording when your time for each one is finished.

Part C – Conversations

Instructions: You will hear conversations between two people, followed by questions. Give a short simple response to each question. When you have finished all the exercises, listen to the recording again and check your answers, using the answer key at the end of the book.

Part D – Sentence Completion

Instructions: Now refer to your test book. Please write one word that best fits the meaning of each sentence. On the real test, you will see the sentences on the computer screen and type in your response. The beeps on the recording indicate the time allowed for each one. You should play the recording as you write your answers.

1. Ted enjoys singing, as _____ as dancing.

2. You're walking too _____ . Please slow down.

3. I slept to long this morning and was _____ for work.

4. To _____ for that job, you need to have a degree from a college or university.

5. I need to _____ the post office of my new address.

6. I told him I would pick him _____ this morning in my car.

7. I _____ to his house last weekend.

8. Could you please _____ the window to let in some fresh air?

9. I thought I had lost my keys, but I managed to _____ them later.

10. Let's keep seeing each other every month. I would hate it if we lost _____ with each other.

11. He _____ his English placement exam, but hopes to pass it the next time.

12. All of the employees were gathered around the table to discuss the project at the team _____ .

13. He had a nice job and a good income, but then he got _____ off.

14. We need to _____ this invoice by the end of the week to avoid the late fee.

15. If you are not in support of the plan, then you must be _____ it.

16. The company policy says that all employees need to _____ a uniform.

17. The result _____ the discussion was that the company decided to hire more staff.

18. You will need to show respect _____ your boss to succeed at work.

Part E – Dictation

Instructions: Now open the word processor program on your computer. You will hear 14 sentences. Type each sentence on your computer exactly as you hear it in the time provided on the recording.

Part F – Passage Reconstruction

Instructions: For this part of the test, you will see two paragraphs. You will have 30 seconds to read each one. After 30 seconds, the paragraph will disappear from your screen. You then need to re-write the passage, using your own words in the time allowed on the recording. For this practice test, you should leave your test book open to Part F of the test and type your answer into a word processing program. You will be allowed 90 seconds to rewrite each of the passages. Please listen to the recording for the timings of the reading and the writing sections.

DO NOT LOOK AT THE PARAGRAPHS AS YOU RE-WRITE THEM!

Paragraph 1:

Martin is 85 years old and lives in a retirement community on the edge of town. He enjoys his life there, although he occasionally feels lonely because his children can't visit as often as he would like. He eats meals with the other residents every day, and he has commented that the food is pretty good. The nurses that work there are also very caring.

Paragraph 2:

Bart was dreaming of his vacation in Costa Rica. He loved adventure, and was going to go water skiing and mountain climbing while he was there. However, the day before he was going to go away, he had an accident on his motorcycle and broke his leg. He hopes that he'll be able to go to Costa Rica next year.

Versant 4-Skills Practice Test 8

Part A – Repeat

Instructions: You will hear sixteen sentences or questions. Repeat each one word for word in the time allowed on the recording.

Part B – Sentence Builds

Instructions: You will hear three groups of words in an incorrect order. After you hear them, say the sentence or question with the words in the correct order. You will hear a beep on your recording when your time for each one is finished.

Part C – Conversations

Instructions: You will hear conversations between two people, followed by questions. Give a short simple response to each question. When you have finished all the exercises, listen to the recording again and check your answers, using the answer key at the end of the book.

Part D – Sentence Completion

Instructions: Now refer to your test book. Please write one word that best fits the meaning of each sentence. On the real test, you will see the sentences on the computer screen and type in your response. The beeps on the recording indicate the time allowed for each one. You should play the recording as you write your answers.

1. It is _____ outside today, so I don't think I'll need a sweater.

2. She works really slowly, so I _____ that she'll finish the job on time.

3. The man was shouting and screaming, but people took no _____ of him.

4. The company policy has _____ recently regarding time off.

5. Could I have a smaller _____ of cake please?

6. Will you please turn _____ the TV? I'd like to watch it.

7. My bus was delayed in traffic, so I _____ late.

8. If you make a _____, then you should clean it up yourself.

9. I hope to go on _____ to California next year.

10. They didn't have the item, but they said it would be _____ next week.

11. I would prefer to speak to someone in _____, rather than over the phone.

12. We need to _____ all staff that the store will be closed next week.

13. I need a _____ cable because this one is too long.

14. The document was placed in the wrong mail box _____ mistake.

15. I am completely fed up _____ this terrible situation.

16. The store doesn't accept credit cards. You will need to pay in _____.

17. It is so noisy in the next room. We should tell them to be _____ .

18. I don't think you will get away _____ leaving work early every day.

Part E – Dictation

Instructions: Now open the word processor program on your computer. You will hear 14 sentences. Type each sentence on your computer exactly as you hear it in the time provided on the recording.

Part F – Passage Reconstruction

Instructions: For this part of the test, you will see two paragraphs. You will have 30 seconds to read each one. After 30 seconds, the paragraph will disappear from your screen. You then need to re-write the passage, using your own words in the time allowed on the recording. For this practice test, you should leave your test book open to Part F of the test and type your answer into a word processing program. You will be allowed 90 seconds to rewrite each of the passages. Please listen to the recording for the timings of the reading and the writing sections.

DO NOT LOOK AT THE PARAGRAPHS AS YOU RE-WRITE THEM!

Paragraph 1:

Frankie wanted to buy a new car and had been looking for one for a few weeks. She looked at all of the ads in the newspaper and online, and had been to visit a few car salespeople. She finally bought what she thought was the perfect one on the internet. It was a small red car, with a big engine, which would be perfect for getting around in the traffic.

Paragraph 2:

George was hoping for a change at work and applied for a job to teach new employees how to use the company's computer system. He was already working in the company's computer department, but with online security. He found that job a bit boring because he didn't see anyone all day long. He now meets new employees every day and is much happier.

Versant 4-Skills Practice Test 9

Part A – Repeat

Instructions: You will hear sixteen sentences or questions. Repeat each one word for word in the time allowed on the recording.

Part B – Sentence Builds

Instructions: You will hear three groups of words in an incorrect order. After you hear them, say the sentence or question with the words in the correct order. You will hear a beep on your recording when your time for each one is finished.

Part C – Conversations

Instructions: You will hear conversations between two people, followed by questions. Give a short simple response to each question. When you have finished all the exercises, listen to the recording again and check your answers, using the answer key at the end of the book.

Part D – Sentence Completion

Instructions: Now refer to your test book. Please write one word that best fits the meaning of each sentence. On the real test, you will see the sentences on the computer screen and type in your response. The beeps on the recording indicate the time allowed for each one. You should play the recording as you write your answers.

1. He is far _____ stupid. In fact, he is the most intelligent person I know.

2. This coat is really _____. I would like a cheaper one.

3. That restaurant is really busy, so you will need to make a _____ if you want to eat there.

4. She was sitting _____ them, with Cindy on her left and Ian on her right.

5. The lecture was so dull that I thought I was going to fall _____ .

6. I often have _____ with getting to sleep at night, especially when I'm worried about something.

7. He never quite got _____ their argument and continues to be upset about it.

8. He wanted to lose weight and decided to _____ more.

9. My watch is broken. Could you tell me the _____ please?

10. If you are _____, you should have something to eat.

11. Entering the museum is _____ . You don't need to pay anything.

12. My grandma is coming to visit me _____ the beginning of the month.

13. If she is asking you too many questions, tell her to mind her own _____ .

14. They disagree with the plan, and they are going to _____ to it at the next meeting.

15. How is everything _____ for you with your new job?

16. The manager needs to sign the document to show that she _____ of it.

17. What you have requested is impossible. I mean, it's really out of the _____.

18. She had a bad accident, but the doctor said she will pull _____ and recover from her injuries.

Part E – Dictation

Instructions: Now open the word processor program on your computer. You will hear 14 sentences. Type each sentence on your computer exactly as you hear it in the time provided on the recording.

Part F – Passage Reconstruction

Instructions: For this part of the test, you will see two paragraphs. You will have 30 seconds to read each one. After 30 seconds, the paragraph will disappear from your screen. You then need to re-write the passage, using your own words in the time allowed on the recording. For this practice test, you should leave your test book open to Part F of the test and type your answer into a word processing program. You will be allowed 90 seconds to rewrite each of the passages. Please listen to the recording for the timings of the reading and the writing sections.

DO NOT LOOK AT THE PARAGRAPHS AS YOU RE-WRITE THEM!

Paragraph 1:

Ray and Nancy's little boy was going to attend a children's party. All of the children were supposed to wear costumes to the party, and it was going to be a lot of fun. The couple took their boy to the store to get him a special outfit, and he chose a pirate costume. He really loved the costume, especially the special hat that came with it.

Paragraph 2:

Rosa loves doing gardening in her backyard and likes growing several different kinds of flowers. Every morning, she goes outside to put water on the plants and care for them. Occasionally, she cuts some flowers and puts them in a vase on her table to enjoy inside the house. She really thinks that gardening is a wonderful hobby.

Versant 4-Skills Practice Test 10

Part A – Repeat

Instructions: You will hear sixteen sentences or questions. Repeat each one word for word in the time allowed on the recording.

Part B – Sentence Builds

Instructions: Rearrange the word groups into a sentence. On the real test, you will hear the word groups on the recording one by one. After each one, you need to speak into the microphone, saying the correct sentence.

Part C – Conversations

Instructions: You will hear conversations between two people, followed by questions. Give a short simple response to each question. When you have finished all the exercises, listen to the recording again and check your answers, using the answer key at the end of the book.

Part D – Sentence Completion

Instructions: Now refer to your test book. Please write one word that best fits the meaning of each sentence. On the real test, you will see the sentences on the computer screen and type in your response. The beeps on the recording indicate the time allowed for each one. You should play the recording as you write your answers.

1. If you are out alone at night, you need to look _____ for danger.

2. My parents _____ each other for the first time when they were at college.

3. She is a lot of _____ because she is always telling jokes.

4. If you _____ more money than you have, you might get into debt.

5. The economy is going to _____ from the serious recession last year.

6. I don't need that anymore. You can _____ it away.

7. The weather was bad, so we _____ our picnic until next week.

8. I am in a hurry, so I don't have _____ to talk now.

9. The new machinery was expensive, but the cost seems to have been _____ it so far.

10. She was really happy _____ getting the big promotion.

11. There has been a mix up. I need to _____ things right.

12. If you hadn't eaten so much, you wouldn't have gotten a _____ ache.

13. You're a fool if you believe her because she has _____ us many lies.

14. I didn't _____ on seeing him. Running into him was a coincidence.

15. I have no _____ where your book is. It could be anywhere.

16. He is unwell. In fact, he's been feeling _____ the weather for a few days.

17. The report showed better results than anyone _____.

18. Many people feel shy about _____ in a foreign language.

Part E – Dictation

Instructions: Now open the word processor program on your computer. You will hear 14 sentences. Type each sentence on your computer exactly as you hear it in the time provided on the recording.

Part F – Passage Reconstruction

Instructions: For this part of the test, you will see two paragraphs. You will have 30 seconds to read each one. After 30 seconds, the paragraph will disappear from your screen. You then need to re-write the passage, using your own words in the time allowed on the recording. For this practice test, you should leave your test book open to Part F of the test and type your answer into a word processing program. You will be allowed 90 seconds to rewrite each of the passages. Please listen to the recording for the timings of the reading and the writing sections.

DO NOT LOOK AT THE PARAGRAPHS AS YOU RE-WRITE THEM!

Paragraph 1:

After living in a small apartment in the city for ten years, Darleen decided to buy a big house in the country. She was really looking forward to living there, and she thought that she was finally going to be able to get a dog and a cat, and maybe even a horse. However, when Darleen moved to the new house, she didn't like it because it felt far away and lonely. So, she decided to move back into the city.

Paragraph 2:

Tony works in a busy office, preparing documents for a lawyer. He works on a complicated computer system that has access to all of the laws and regulations. He was working on a big project one day, when the computer system went down. Tony's boss was angry when he didn't have the documents ready, but then Tony explained to him that the computer system hadn't been working, and his boss apologized.

Additional Information and Test Questions for Amazon, Deloitte, & MNCs

The Versant Test for Amazon, Deloitte, and certain multi-national corporations (MNCs) consists of the following sections:

Typing
You will be shown a passage and asked to type as many words of it as you can in 60 seconds. Your score will be given based on how quickly you type, as well as how many mistakes you have made.

Additional exercises for typing are provided in the next section of the book.

Complete the Sentence
You will read a short sentence, and you will need to put a word into it to complete it.

This is the same as Part D of the practice tests in this book.

Dictation
You will listen to sentences and type what you have heard.

This is the same as Part E of the practice tests in this book.

Reconstruct the Paragraph
You will read a paragraph in the 30 seconds allowed. Then you will have 90 seconds to write your own version of the paragraph.

This is the same as Part F of the practice tests in this book.

Email Writing
You will need to write a brief email of about 100 words in response to the scenario provided.

Email writing exercises are given after the Typing exercises in the next section.

Typing Exercises

Typing Exercise 1

Instructions: Accurately type as much of the passage below as you can in 60 seconds. For the time limits, please open the audio entitled "Typing" at:

test-prep-guides.com/versant-test-practice-online/4-skills-professional-essential/

Credit card debt is a major cause of over one million bankruptcies each year. The reason is that many people get a credit card without researching and reading the fine print. By the time annual fees are added on, along with spending indiscriminately, payments are missed, which causes balances to skyrocket. Although we all like to place the blame on the credit cards and the credit card companies, individuals themselves are the real culprits. In short, if a person's credit card spending is out of control, they need to keep in mind that the real cause of the financial mess is a lack of self-discipline. If a person can summon enough willpower and strength to manage their finances and spending, then they will find be winners in the game of finance. It may be easy to get into debt, but getting out of debt is much more difficult.

Typing Exercise 2

Instructions: Accurately type as much of the passage below as you can in 60 seconds. For the time limits, please open the audio entitled "Typing" at:

test-prep-guides.com/versant-test-practice-online/4-skills-professional-essential/

A complex series of interactive patterns govern nearly everything the human body does. We eat to a rhythm and drink, sleep, and even breathe to separate ones. Research shows that the human body clock is affected by three main rhythmic cycles: the rhythm at which the earth revolves on its axis, the monthly revolution of the moon around the earth, and the annual revolution of the earth around the sun. These natural rhythms, sometimes called circadian rhythms, are partially controlled by the hypothalamus in the brain. Circadian rhythms help to explain the "lark vs. owl" hypothesis These cycles also explain the phenomenon of jet lag, when the individual's body clock is out of step with the actual clock time in his or her new location in the world. In humans, births and deaths also follow predictable cycles, with most births and deaths occurring between midnight and 6:00 am.

Typing Exercise 3

Instructions: Accurately type as much of the passage below as you can in 60 seconds. For the time limits, please open the audio entitled "Typing" at:

test-prep-guides.com/versant-test-practice-online/4-skills-professional-essential/

Diners in restaurants sometimes ask why their servers aren't able to cope with some of their requests. Is it fair to suggest that members of the service industry typically deliver below-par service to customers? Consider a simple example of a fast-food restaurant. Chances are that you've been at the receiving end of some bad service at some point in time. Is it then fair to assume that staff that wear work uniforms are simply to be tagged with a warning sign that they will not deliver to their clientele? To understand the reasons for occasional bad service, the factors influencing the situation need to be considered. Perhaps the person providing the service was new to his or her job. Maybe he or she was a trainee and was not able to perform without the assistance of a supervisor. In addition, service people can experience a great deal of stress when trying to do several things at once for different patrons.

Typing Exercise 4

Instructions: Accurately type as much of the passage below as you can in 60 seconds. For the time limits, please open the audio entitled "Typing" at:

test-prep-guides.com/versant-test-practice-online/4-skills-professional-essential/

"Celebrity" is the term used to describe someone who is famous and attracts attention from the general public and the world's media. Traditionally, a celebrity would gain the title by his or her work or achievements in a particular field of expertise. Actors, musicians, politicians, and inventors have all become celebrities in the past. However, as we move more deeply into the twenty-first century, a new celebrity has arrived – the nobody. As one peruses glossy TV magazines, it is easy to notice the amount of reality shows that have dominated our screens – Wife Swap, X-Factor, American Idol, America's Got Talent, and the reality pioneer Big Brother. The concept itself of Big Brother is everything that George Orwell warned us about: "normal" people are thrust into the limelight to be mocked, glorified, vilified, and humiliated in equal measures.

Typing Exercise 5

Instructions: Accurately type as much of the passage below as you can in 60 seconds. For the time limits, please open the audio entitled "Typing" at:

test-prep-guides.com/versant-test-practice-online/4-skills-professional-essential/

Almost everyone has heard the song "Don't Worry, Be Happy" by Bobby McFerrin. The song has a very repetitive way of conveying its message. McFerrin's refrain was that everyone can feel happy if they simply choose not to worry. Living a happy and worry-free life is a wonderful ideal, but it must be said that life is full of stresses and strains that are often not of our own choosing. One of the truest things ever said is that the only thing in life that will always remain the same is change. In addition to causing us to worry, stress is also linked to the top causes of death, such as heart disease, cancer, and stroke. So, achieving happiness in today's society is often a complex, multi-dimensional process.

Email Exercises

Email Exercise 1

Instructions: Read the information below and write a 100-word or more email in response to the situation. For the time limit, please open the audio entitled "Email Writing" at:

test-prep-guides.com/versant-test-practice-online/4-skills-professional-essential/

You are the manager of a data processing company. Staff members have been working very hard this year and have achieved all of their targets. However, the company had higher expenses this year, so it won't be able to pay bonuses.

Write an email to staff conveying this information and suggesting the following options for rewards for all staff instead:
- A meal out
- A company picnic
- A one-month membership to an online movie network

The reward will be chosen based upon the highest number of staff member preferences for the option.

A sample response is provided on the next page.

To: All Staff

From: Data Processing Manager

Re: Year-end Bonuses

Dear Staff:

First of all, I wanted to give sincere thanks on behalf of the company for everyone's hard work this year. Your performance has been excellent and senior management is especially pleased that all targets have been reached. Unfortunately, it's my responsibility to let you know that our expenses were much higher his year. For this reason, we won't be able to pay bonuses at year-end.

To show our appreciation, we would like to offer all employees one of the following: a restaurant meal, free membership for a month to an online movie service, or a picnic for all staff. Once we have received input from everyone, we will choose the option that has been the most popular, and let everyone know.

Thanks again for your dedication this past year.

Sincerely,
Henry

Email Exercise 2

Instructions: Read the information below and write a 100-word or more email in response to the situation. For the time limit, please open the audio entitled "Email Writing" at:

test-prep-guides.com/versant-test-practice-online/4-skills-professional-essential/

You are the director of a company that manufactures and ships items overseas. There has been a strike at the port, and this month's shipments are going to be delayed.

Write an email to all department managers about the situation, and propose suggestions. Your suggestions must come from the following list:
- Cut manufacturing this month
- Send the items by air
- Hire workers at the port to try to break the strike

Tell the managers that you are waiting for their feedback.

A sample response is provided on the next page.

To: All Department Managers

From: The Director

Re: Pending Strike Action

Dear Management Team:

The purpose of this email is to inform all department managers that there is going to be a strike at the port this month, which will cause our shipments to be delayed. As you know, we cannot really afford for this to happen. Accordingly, I would like to put forward the following thoughts.

(1) We could decrease our manufacturing output this month, so that fewer items would need to be shipped.
(2) We could send the shipments by air freight instead.
(3) We could hire additional staff to try to break the strike at the port.

As you know, there are advantages and disadvantages to each of these options. I would like to know the thoughts of all department managers on this matter so that we may come to the best course of action for everyone concerned.

Many thanks,
Monica

Email Exercise 3

Instructions: Read the information below and write a 100-word or more email in response to the situation. For the time limit, please open the audio entitled "Email Writing" at:

test-prep-guides.com/versant-test-practice-online/4-skills-professional-essential/

You are the manager of an accounting firm which is trying to acquire new clients. Clients in the banking, investment, and financial services industries are especially needed.

Send an email to senior accountants at the firm explaining these facts and propose that senior accountants try to gain new clients. Recommendations for obtaining new clients must come from these courses of action:
- Join a local club such as Lions' Club or the Rotary Club
- Attend special networking classes during the next four weekends
- Arrange meetings with friends and acquaintances working in the financial services sector

Individual appointments will be scheduled with each senior accountant to see what they have done or intend to do about this matter.

A sample response is provided on the next page.

To: All Senior Accountants

From: Firm Manager

Re: New Client Acquisition

Dear Senior Accounting Staff:

I wanted to give all of you the details of our big drive for new clients. At present, we are seeking additional clientele, especially those in the financial services, banking, and investment sectors. As senior members of staff, all of you should be striving to add to and build our client portfolio.

The following are examples of what you could do to help us obtain new clients in these areas: join local social or business clubs to liaise with like-mined professionals and obtain new contacts; renew contacts with your acquaintances who are working in financial services to grain trust and see if they have any accountancy needs, or attend classes during the next four weekends to improve your networking skills.

I would like all of you to consider these options. I'll contact each one of you in the near future to schedule an individual appointment to discuss this matter face-to-face.

Thanking you in anticipation,
Margaret

Email Exercise 4

Instructions: Read the information below and write a 100-word or more email in response to the situation. For the time limit, please open the audio entitled "Email Writing" at:

test-prep-guides.com/versant-test-practice-online/4-skills-professional-essential/

You are the line manager for a busy warehouse and shipping facility. Write an email to all line staff to thank them for their achievement this quarter. Then point out the following areas for improvement when fulfilling customer orders:
- Items need to be packaged with more care to avoid damage
- Items need to be picked with great speed
- Less packaging material should be used on large items

A sample response is provided on the next page.

To: All Line Staff

From: Line Manager

Re: Thanks and reminders

Dear Line Staff:

Firstly, thanks for your hard work and cooperation this past quarter. Your dedication was essential in helping us achieve our goals during the past three months, and it was very much appreciated.

In order to continue giving top-notch service to our customers, I'd like to remind you to be especially diligent about the following aspects of order fulfilment going forward:

Please be sure to take care when packaging items to avoid causing any damage to them. Also, please try to select and pick items for an order a bit more quickly wherever possible. Lastly, when packing larger orders, try to cut down on the amount of packaging, unless of course this would cause damage to the order.

Should you have questions or concerns about any of these aspects of order fulfillment, please let me know.

Thanks again,
Thomas

Email Exercise 5

Instructions: Read the information below and write a 100-word or more email in response to the situation. For the time limit, please open the audio entitled "Email Writing" at:

test-prep-guides.com/versant-test-practice-online/4-skills-professional-essential/

You are a supervisor in a call center that takes customer calls from overseas. Customers have complained that call center staff sometimes fail to do the following:
- Speak loudly enough
- Speak clearly
- Spend enough time explaining a problem

Write an email to all staff informing them of these problems and then propose solutions for each of these points.

A sample response is provided on the next page.

To: All Call Center Staff

From: Call Center Supervisor

Re: Customer feedback

Dear Staff:

Thanks to all of you for your efforts in dealing with the multitude of overseas calls that we receive each day with professionalism and patience.

Following customer feedback, I wanted to point out that certain customers have commented that it is sometimes difficult to hear or understand call center staff and that problems have not been explained to the customer in sufficient detail on occasion.

In response to these comments, could I please remind all call center staff always to try to speak in an articulate and clear way, and to be sure to ask the caller if they can hear you speaking. In addition, please remember to ask the customer if everything is clear or if they have any further questions before finishing a call.

If you have any questions or comments about this feedback, please let me know.

Thanks again for your diligence and dedication.

Martina

Additional Practice for the Versant Student Placement Test

Read Aloud

For items 1 to 5, read the text aloud as clearly and as naturally as you can, at a good pace, and with good pronunciation and emphasis. You are given 30 seconds for each item. Please open the mp3 with the instructions entitled "Read Aloud" at:

test-prep-guides.com/versant-test-practice-online/4-skills-professional-essential/

Item 1:

The Scotch philosopher, David Hume, has been called the father of social psychology because of his splendid analysis of sympathy as a social force. However, sympathy is not always limited in its operation to the present moment. Through sympathy we may put ourselves in the future situation of any person whose present condition arouses our interest. Vice was defined by Hume as everything which gives uneasiness in human actions. By sympathy, we become uneasy when we become aware of injustice anywhere. There is a continual conflict between self-interest and sympathy, both in the individual and between individuals in society. Although at times this self-interest seems to predominate, it does not entirely clash with the aims of friendship and goodness. [from *A History of Social Thought*, Emory Bogardus, public domain]

Item 2:

There is a science of getting rich, and it is an exact science, like algebra or arithmetic. There are certain laws which govern the process of acquiring wealth; once these laws are learned and obeyed by any person, they will get rich with mathematical certainty. Those who do things according to these certain laws, whether intentionally or accidentally, will acquire material wealth. Getting rich is not a matter of environment, because if it were, all the people in certain neighborhoods would become affluent; the people of one city would all be living in prosperity, while those of other towns would all be living in poverty. But everywhere we see rich and poor living contemporaneously in the same communities, and often engaged in the same vocations. [from *The Science of Getting Rich*, by W.D. Wattles, public domain]

Item 3:

No extension of foreign trade will immediately increase the amount of value in a country, although it will very powerfully contribute to increase the mass of commodities. As the value of all foreign goods is measured by the quantity of the produce of our land and labor, which is given in exchange for them, we should have no greater value, if by the discovery of new markets, we obtained double the quantity of foreign goods in exchange for a given quantity of ours. It has indeed been contended that the great profits which are sometimes made by particular merchants in foreign trade will elevate the general rate of profits in the country, and that the abstraction of capital from employment to partake of the new and beneficial foreign commerce will raise prices generally, and thereby increase profits. [from *The Principles of Political Economy and Taxation*, David Ricardo, public domain]

Item 4:

A survey of the post office quickly illustrates the fact that it could only be successfully conducted by a cohort agency of skilled employees, specially trained for the work. The distribution of the mail is dependent upon employees who certainly must closely apply themselves to the mastery of the schemes of separation, and we should imagine that these are rather tedious to study, for it seems to be largely a matter of routine and memory regarding absolutely unrelated names and places. It is a work to which a person must devote a good part of their life and must have constant practice in order to maintain the required speed and the duty of standing eight hours a day in front of a case and boxing letters by the thousand, year in and year out. [from *The Postal System of the United States*, Manufacturer's Trust Company, public domain]

Item 5:

The question whether the human race will ever advance far beyond its present position in intellect and morals is one which has engaged much attention. Judging from the past, we cannot reasonably doubt that great advances are yet to be made, but if the principle of development is admitted, advancement is certain, whatever may be the space of time required for its realization. A progression resembling development may be traced in human nature, both in the individual and in large groups of individuals. Not only this, but also by the work of our thoughtful brains and occupied hands, we modify external nature in a way never known before. The physical improvements wrought by humanity upon the earth's surface are for the possible development of higher types of humanity, beings who shall be stronger in intellect and more fit for the demands of social life, because society will, by that point, have less to dread and more to love. [from *The World' Greatest Books – Science*, WMH Wise & Company, public domain]

Summary and Opinion – Item 1

Instructions: Read the passage below. First, write a 25 to 50-word summary of the passage. Then write your opinion on the topic. You must write at least 50 words for the second task. You have 18 minutes to complete these two tasks.

Please open the mp3 with the instructions entitled "Summary and Opinion" at:

test-prep-guides.com/versant-test-practice-online/4-skills-professional-essential/

Internet Communication

Many people believe that the internet is essential for communication in our modern society. On the other hand, there are those who hold the view that the internet contains worthless or offensive information. This essay will show that although the internet needs to be used cautiously in certain circumstances, it also contains some helpful educational materials and factual data.

It is true that internet usage needs to be approached vigilantly on certain occasions. For example, parents worry about children accessing websites that contain violent, illegal, or sexual materials. This, in turn, could negatively influence the formative years of a child's personality development. In addition, some information on the internet needs to be read with a critical mind. The qualifications of the site owner, as well as the accuracy and quality of the information on the site need to be scrutinized skeptically.

In spite of these caveats, the internet is also practical for our daily lives. First of all, it makes some daily tasks more convenient, such as booking airline tickets and making other travel arrangements. There are also websites that contain indispensable factual information. Consider the case of someone who wants to quit smoking. He or she can use any search engine to find webpages that offer help and advice with this situation. In addition, many of these types of websites are established by governmental agencies or charitable organizations, so the user can be confident that the information contained on these webpages is trustworthy.

To sum up, there are of course some situations in which users of the internet need to be prudent. Yet, there are also many helpful and accurate websites as well. It is up to each adult individual or parent, in the case of children, to decide which websites they are going to access.

Item 1 – Sample Responses

Summary

The passage discusses the pro's and con's of internet use. Some of the benefits are that the internet makes certain everyday jobs easier and helps us to find information. On the other hand, the disadvantages are the false materials and the websites that are harmful to children and vulnerable people.

Opinion

I agree with the article that the internet poses both benefits and risks to society. Besides the risks that the passage mentions, we have heard about deadly behaviors that are shown, or even promoted online. Take for example the case of the eating disorder anorexia. A person suffering from this type of illness can easily access pro-ana websites and social media posts that will encourage and support this dangerous behavior. Encouragement of this illness can be deadly. We have also seen similar dangers with pro-suicide websites and social media posts.

Another appalling example is the recent case of the "Blackout Challenge." This challenge, which has been posted on social media, encourages young children to make themselves pass out. However, what the children do not realize is that they may actually suffocate or strangle themselves to death in trying to compete in this so-called "challenge."

In terms of positive aspects to the internet, however, I would like to speak about educational materials. When I was preparing for this exam, for instance, I was able to find a number of coaching sites on line, as well as educational videos on YouTube. These materials greatly assisted me in improving my English language skills and helped me to prepare for the examination.

So, just like the article says, we need to be inquisitive when we read information online. This means sometimes asking questions about the veracity and authenticity of the material, as well as knowing when to report harmful information to a platform provider.

Summary and Opinion – Item 2

Instructions: Read the passage below. First, write a 25 to 50-word summary of the passage. Then write your opinion on the topic. You must write at least 50 words for the second task. You have 18 minutes to complete these two tasks.

Please open the mp3 with the instructions entitled "Summary and Opinion" at:

test-prep-guides.com/versant-test-practice-online/4-skills-professional-essential/

Electronics Recycling:

Many cities, towns, and villages around the world are becoming increasingly vigilant about computer and television recycling in order to protect the environment and avoid possible soil contamination. Because computers contain many parts that can readily release toxins into the soil, city governments are seeking alternative ways to dispose of antiquated computers and other types of discarded electronic equipment. In my opinion, this eventually should become a normal practice, with more cities becoming aware of the potential danger of disposing of computers and other electronic products in landfills. Activist groups are also rightly informing the public about computer recycling and are researching new and better ways to dispose of electronic equipment.

In many cities, local electronic stores or recycling centers will take disused computers and other electronics, dismantle them, and place the parts into the correct containers for disposal. This method of disposal has become a necessity on a global scale as the computer industry perpetually upgrades operating systems, in effect establishing "enforced obsolescence" whereby consumers need to replace old computers in order to keep their equipment and related software up-to-date. Because obsolete computers continue to be placed into landfills as they have in the past, this situation has created environmental issues that need to be addressed by the government. Therefore, we all need to do our part to bring awareness to environmental issues urgently now, even if it means resorting to extreme or illegal measures, like participating in protests or civil unrest.

Item 2 – Sample Responses

Summary

Recycling is a big issue for our modern society, especially considering the electronics that have been dumped in landfills around the world. The article discusses the different types of recycling programs that are available, and concludes that we need to take radical or even illegal action to prevent more damage to the environment.

Opinion

I agree with the article to an extent, although I could never condone illegal acts, like the article suggests. It is true that there already are a great deal of dumped electronic devices causing environmental damage around the world. People should be more motivated to recycle their electronic items, but sometimes the cost or inconvenience get in the way of their otherwise good intentions. For instance, I have travelled both to England and to the United States recently, and have seen illegal dumping of items like refrigerators or televisions by the side of the road or in wooded areas. Ostensibly, people do this because of the cost involved in disposing of the items properly. Or perhaps a more cynical person might even say that people are simply too lazy sometimes to do the right thing.

I also completely support the statement that computer companies basically force us to dispose of our old computers. For example, the software provider for my PC recently informed me that they would no longer be offering support for the operating system used on my computer. So, I can only imagine that when my computer eventually breaks down, it will be quite difficult to find someone who will be able to repair it, and I may then need to get rid of it.

Where I differ from the passage is in the belief that illegal or extreme actions need to be taken in order to protect the environment. I do believe that we all need to do our part to solve this problem, but would only support legal measures, such as the signing of petitions, speaking with governmental representatives, or participating in peaceful marches.

APPENDIX 1

For the audio recordings that accompany these practice tests, please go to:

https://test-prep-guides.com/versant-test-practice-online/4-skills-professional-essential/

ANSWER KEYS

Versant 4-Skills Practice Test 1

Test 1 Part A – Repeat

1. Do you know what's wrong with the printer?

2. Where is the company's mail room?

3. You are allowed 30 minutes for a lunch break.

4. I'm pretty sure that we can meet the deadline.

5. You can count on me.

6. Here is my business card, so be sure to call.

7. The files for the company are on the external drive.

8. Please put that letter back on my desk.

9. The train station is at the end of this road.

10. You need to ask permission to leave work early.

11. I need to stop at the store on the way home.

12. I left my umbrella on the train.

13. The discount doesn't apply to postage and packaging costs.

14. The new computer system is very efficient and powerful.

15. All employees will be assigned additional duties.

16. It is company policy that uniforms should always be cleaned and pressed.

Test 1 Part B – Sentence Builds

1. anything / see / I didn't

   Answer: I didn't see anything.

2. of his / she is / a friend

    Answer: She is a friend of his.

3. you here / to see / I never expected

    Answer: I never expected to see you here.

4. my little sister / to see / I'm going

    Answer: I going to see my little sister.

5. the train / thirty minutes late / had arrived

    Answer: The train had arrived thirty minutes late.

6. project is / due today / that important

    Answer: That important project is due today.

7. more sales / to make / we hope

    Answer: We hope to make more sales.

8. a recent report / in detail / described the findings

    Answer: A recent report described the findings in detail.

Test 1 Part C – Conversations

Conversation 1:
Where are my keys?
They're right beside the newspaper.
Okay. Thanks!
Where are the woman's keys?
Answer: beside the newspaper

Conversation 2:
Are you from Boston?
Yes, my family still lives there.
It's so much nicer than New York.
Where does the man's family live?
Answer: in Boston

Conversation 3:
Would you like to come to the movie with me?
I can't. I'm expecting a delivery.
Never mind. I understand.
Why can't the woman go to the movie?
Answer: She is expecting a delivery.

Conversation 4:
I want to eat a cheeseburger.
Are you going to get something to drink with it?
Lemonade would be great.
What will the woman order to drink?
Answer: a lemonade

Conversation 5:
Do you give any money to charity?
I do. I donate to the Cancer Society.
That's really great.
Where does the man donate?
Answer: to the Cancer Society

Conversation 6:
Let's meet in front of the cafe on Saturday.
Sounds good to me. What time?
At 3 o'clock.
Where will they meet on Saturday?
Answer: in front of the cafe

Conversation 7:
Can I bring something to your house dinner?
Could you bring some butter for the bread?
Sure. No problem.
What will the man bring?
Answer: butter for the bread

Conversation 8:
I'm going to have to change my travel plans.
Why's that?
I need to leave a couple of days later.
What does the man need to change?
Answer: his travel plans

Conversation 9
I finished cleaning the house already.
How did you get it done so quickly?
I did part of it yesterday.
What did the woman finish?
Answer: cleaning the house

Conversation 10:
They should be done with the garden on Monday.
That seems impossible. There's still a lot left to do.
I know. I think so too.
What should be done on Monday?
Answer: They should be done with the garden.

Conversation 11:
My toilet doesn't work.
Have you said anything to your landlord?
Yes, he's sending a plumber to repair it tonight.
What problem did the woman tell her landlord about?
Answer: that the toilet wasn't working / didn't work

Conversation 12:
Where's the nearest exit?
There's one next to the elevator.
Okay. Thanks.
What is located next to the elevator?
Answer: the nearest exit

Test 1 Part D – Sentence Completion

1. You're driving too _____ . We're going to be late. **slowly**

2. I need to pick up some medicine at the _____ . **pharmacy / chemist**

3. I went to the supermarket yesterday to _____ some food. **get / buy / purchase**

4. The woman _____ her eyeglasses and had to buy a new pair. **lost / misplaced / mislaid**

5. For more _____ about the job, please see the advertisement online. **information**

6. The return _____ needs to be provided on that letter. **address**

7. We need to touch _____, so give me a call tomorrow. **base** (Note: "Touch base" is an idiom that means to get in contact with someone.)

8. Even though she failed her last driving test, she had high _____ that she would pass this time. **hopes**

9. I _____ up early this morning, so I had breakfast early. **got / woke**

10. You need to make an _____ if you would like to speak to the Director. **appointment**

11. He was assistant manager, but now he has been _____ to manager. **promoted**

12. They _____ a mistake in how they spelled my name. **made**

13. Although you don't _____ with his methods, we still have to follow his instructions. **agree**

14. You need to use that _____ to unlock the door. **key**

15. The college _____ a wide range of classes for the young and old alike. **offers**

16. The company caused the pollution, so they need to _____ the cost of the clean-up themselves. **cover** (Note that "pay" is incorrect because you would need to say "pay for.")

17. Employees will lose pay accordingly if they are _____ to work. **late**

18. I can finally relax now that the big project has reached an _____ . **end**

Test 1 Part E – Dictation

1. It will be ready on Monday.

2. I wish that we didn't have so much work to do.

3. It's a good idea to be attentive at meetings.

4. Where did you put the keys?

5. There is going to be a party on Friday to celebrate our success.

6. I go to the park every day.

7. You need to make sure that everything is ready for production.

8. The boss told me that they are doing everything they can.

9. If you plan on attending the event, please reply to this email.

10. The bus stops here every fifteen minutes.

11. The company is watching its staffing and materials costs.

12. It's a nice day to be outside.

13. The agreement will be drawn up by the legal department.

14. Companies can apply for certain tax credits and incentives.

Test 1 Part F – Passage Reconstruction (Sample responses)

Paul retired after working for 40 years. For a while, things were fine and he played golf and spent time with his wife. Then he became bored, and told he wife he'd like something to do in his free time. He started volunteering for a charity a couple of days each week, and he really likes it.

Matt told all of his co-workers about a secret surprise party for Liz that he was organizing. Their boss sent a fake email to Liz to say that she had to go to the conference room for an exit interview since she was leaving the company. There were refreshments there, and her co-workers all brought farewell gifts for her and waited for her to arrive. When she entered the room, she saw everyone gathered there.

Versant 4-Skills Practice Test 2 – Answers

Test 2 Part A – Repeat

1. Are you sure it's not a problem?

2. The copy machine is broken again.

3. I'll send the document to you by mail.

4. I always arrive a little early for work.

5. All employees are allowed to wear casual clothes on Friday.

6. Are you free to talk now?

7. I forgot to bring my phone with me today.

8. I'm afraid I'm busy with other things right now.

9. Could I please have your contact information?

10. After he had all the facts, he ended up changing his opinion.

11. Please put the file back in the cabinet when you are finished.

12. She's just stepped out. Can I take a message?

13. How many employees are going to go to the conference?

14. I'm not reading that book, so you can borrow it.

15. Just tell my assistant, and he'll take care of it.

16. I've been having some problems with my computer today.

Test 2 Part B – Sentence Builds

1. this credit card / next month / expires

   Answer: This credit card expires next month.

2. to his car / we didn't see / what happened

   Answer: We didn't see what happened to his car.

3. I was / meeting the president / really happy about

   Answer: I was really happy about meeting the president.

4. someone else / let's choose / to lead the group

   Answer: Let's choose someone else to lead the group.

5. how many points / to win / do you need

    Answer: How many points do you need to win?

6. the parking lot / cars / is full of

   Answer: The parking lot is full of cars.

7. she quit / last week / her management job

   Answer: She quit her management job last week.

8. will be sent / the document / by email

   Answer: The document will be sent by email.

Test 2 Part C – Conversations

Conversation 1:
When are you going to take vacation?
During July.
Me too.
In what month are they going on vacation?
Answer: July

Conversation 2:
You need to sign this form.
Can I borrow your pen?
Okay, here you go.
What does the man borrow from the woman?
Answer: her pen

Conversation 3:
Do you want to go to that new restaurant on Sunday?
I went there for supper last night.

61

Did you enjoy it?
Where does the woman want to go on Sunday?
Answer: that new restaurant

Conversation 4:
Can I read your magazine?
Yes, when I'm finished with it.
Thanks! It looks really interesting.
What item does the woman want to read?
Answer: the magazine

Conversation 5:
Why are you studying?
I have to take my English test tomorrow.
Oh yes, I remember.
What test does the man have tomorrow?
Answer: his English test

Conversation 6:
That new restaurant at the end of the road is advertised in the paper.
I saw it. It says they make pizza over a fire.
Maybe we should eat there this week.
What is advertised about the new restaurant?
Answer: They make pizza over a fire.

Conversation 7:
How was your trip?
A little tiring. The flight was delayed four hours.
That sounds exhausting.
Why is the woman so tired?
Answer: Her flight was delayed.

Conversation 8:
It's so noisy here today.
I know. They are having the town fair.
Oh, that's why.
Why is it noisy?
Answer: They are having the town fair.

Conversation 9:
What was that phone call all about?
It was a school teacher. She wants to bring some children for a tour tomorrow.
I hope they find it interesting.
Who was the woman speaking to on the telephone?
Answer: a school teacher

Conversation 10:
The company's profits aren't good.
I know. I'm quite worried.
Me too.
What are the man and woman worried about?
Answer: The company's profits aren't good.

Conversation 11:
What's your opinion of the new system?
Can I be honest?
Of course. That's why I wanted to ask you.
What does the woman want to know from the man?
Answer: his opinion about the new system

Conversation 12:
Any news about our promotions?
Not yet, but I'll let you know.
Well, let's hope we get them.
What are the two people speaking about?
Answer: news about their promotions

Test 2 Part D – Sentence Completion

1. It is so bright and clear today. There isn't a _____ in the sky. **cloud**

2. I highly _____ her for the job because she is intelligent and attentive. **recommend**

3. To _____ Dan's birthday, his friends are going to have a party. **celebrate**

4. She was _____ from the New York branch to the Los Angeles branch. **transferred**

5. Is this dress available in a smaller _____ ? This one is too big. **size**

6. Will you please turn the lights _____ ? I want to go to sleep. **off**

63

7. He arrived at the airport late, and _____ his flight, so he had to travel the next day. **missed**

8. To avoid the danger from high winds, everyone was told to leave town _____ the hurricane arrived. **before**

9. I went on a _____ of London on a double-decker bus to go sightseeing. **tour**

10. Because of the sale, the bookstore didn't have any more televisions in _____, but they will get another delivery tomorrow. **stock**

11. To get the new product, you can _____ your order online or over the telephone. **place / make**

12. I'm sorry to inform you of this at such short _____, but everyone is going to need to work late tonight. **notice**

13. Their wedding photographer was an _____, not a professional. All of their photographs turned out badly. **amateur**

14. There has been peace _____ the two nations since they signed the international treaty. **between**

15. We thought she would be _____ about going abroad, but she seemed completely bored. **excited**

16. The company was having cash flow problems and had to take out a _____ from the bank. **loan**

17. The next _____ of that product is arriving into port next week. **shipment**

18. He is suffering _____ a strange illness and has been in the hospital for three weeks. **from**

Test 2 Part E – Dictation

1. I hope to be finished by the weekend.

2. Where did you leave your jacket?

3. Sorry, but I haven't been informed about the plans yet.

4. Could you just wait a moment until I've finished speaking?

5. She enjoys going out with friends.

6. The inspection is going to take place at the end of this month.

7. To control its debt, the company has decided to limit its spending.

8. The company hasn't expanded as much as they'd hoped.

9. It seemed like the right thing to do at the time.

10. In my opinion, I don't think we should go ahead.

11. The price is determined by the cost of production.

12. Could I please have some more coffee?

13. I am going to have a day off next week.

14. The boss said she needs the report by Friday.

Test 2 Part F – Passage Reconstruction (Sample responses)

A reminder was sent to all employees about their summer vacation days. They were told to book their vacation days well ahead of time. They were reminded that many employees prefer to take time off in the summer, so the ability to take time off at that time may be limited. To request the vacation days, the employees need to fill in a form and get it approved by their supervisor. The policy will be in effect for June, July, and August to reduce any problems with conflicting vacation schedules.

Shanika got a new doorbell that had a video feature, and she was looking forward to putting it in when she got home. Then she tried to install it, but she discovered that it wouldn't function. So that same day, she went back to the store to return it and get a different one. The sales assistant told her that the doorbell needed batteries put in it in order to work. Shanika hadn't remembered to do this, and she felt embarrassed.

Versant 4-Skills Practice Test 3 – Answers

Test 3 Part A – Repeat

1. Let's eat at the new restaurant on the way home.

2. Is there a special phone number for customer services?

3. We need to get this done by Friday at the latest.

4. It will take nine more months to finish the inside of the building.

5. He just wanted to check in to see whether there had been any improvement.

6. Shipping and handling cost an additional ten dollars.

7. She is able to repair almost anything.

8. Representatives may not share their personal information with customers.

9. They are creating a model for a new, more powerful system.

10. The conference room is becoming very disorganized.

11. Are you going to apply for a new job?

12. He's worked for the same company for almost twenty years.

13. We wanted to thank everyone for a job well done.

14. I'll have another assignment for you on Monday.

15. The issue is a low priority right now.

16. I've been meaning to speak to her about that.

Test 3 Part B – Sentence Builds

1. is he / where / going

   Answer: Where is he going?

2. the weather / tomorrow / will be awful

   Answer: The weather tomorrow will be awful.

3. where should / on vacation / we go

   Answer: Where should we go on vacation?

4. a lot of mistakes / there were / in the report

   Answer: There were a lot of mistakes in the report.

5. did you hear / the company / that she bought

   Answer: Did you hear that she bought the company?

6. when the meeting ended / thanked everyone / the director

   Answer: When the meeting ended, the director thanked everyone. / The director thanked everyone when the meeting ended.

7. were very cheap / all of the items / that were on sale

   Answer: All of the items that were on sale were very cheap.

8. to remove the paper / of the printer / open the top

   Answer: To remove the paper, open the top of the printer / Open the top of the printer to remove the paper.

Test 3 Part C – Conversations

Conversation 1:
This coffee is far too hot.
It must have been left on the heat too long.
Let's add some cold water.
What is too hot?
Answer: the coffee

Conversation 2:
What's the weather forecast for Saturday?
They said it's going to rain all day.
We'll have to cancel the picnic then.
What will the weather be like on Saturday?
Answer: It's going to rain all day.

Conversation 3:
I just got a birthday gift from my brother.
That's nice. What did he give you?
A really interesting book.
What did the man get from his brother?
Answer: a birthday gift / a really interesting book

Conversation 4:
Please write your name and address on this document.
Why do I need to do that?
In case you want to ask for a refund.
What does the man ask the woman to do?
Answer: write down her name and address

Conversation 5:
How's that report going?
I thought maybe you could help me with it.
Sorry, but I don't have time.
What doesn't the man have time to do?
Answer: help the woman with the report

Conversation 6:
Are you going to the concert this weekend?
Yes, I managed to get tickets.
Wow! That's great!
What will the woman do this weekend?
Answer: She's going to the concert.

Conversation 7:
My computer crashed again.
Oh, how awful!
I know. I hope I get it running again soon.
What problem does the man have?
Answer: his computer has crashed

Conversation 8:
Is your son going to go to college?
Yes, he hopes to start next month.
That's good to hear.
What will the woman's son do next month?
Answer: go to college

Conversation 9:
We need to really work hard on this project.
Yes, I think it's going to take some overtime.
Well, the important thing is to finish on time.
Why do the two people need to work hard?
Answer: to finish the project on time

Conversation 10:
The meeting finished quite early.
I was surprised about that too.
We went through all of the points really quickly.
Why are the man and the woman surprised?
Answer: the meeting finished early / the points were covered quickly

Conversation 11:
He's been working really hard lately.
He's got that important deadline coming up.
I hope he gets his work done on time.
Why has he been working hard?
Answer: he has an important deadline coming up

Conversation 12:
Why aren't you going to come on the trip with us?
The truth is, I'm just about out of money.
What happened?
What is the man unable to do?
Answer: go on the trip

Test 3 Part D – Sentence Completion

1. Our manager told us that we will need to work harder than ever to _____ our target this month. **meet / reach / achieve**

2. I need to _____ our reservation at the restaurant since we'll be getting there an hour later. **change**

3. The teacher divided the work for the class project _____ all the students. **among** (Note that "between" is incorrect because "students" is plural.)

4. The workshop was very boring. I really didn't _____ it at all. **like / enjoy**

5. I _____ very deeply at night, and I have extremely vivid dreams. **sleep**

6. It looks like it's going to _____, so I'd better take an umbrella. **rain**

7. Research shows that the viewing _____ of television owners have changed recently. **habits / behaviors**

8. What is today's _____ ? I don't have a calendar. **date**

9. I haven't had anything to drink since this morning, so I'm really _____. **thirsty**

10. Driving on that road isn't free. You need to pay a _____ at the booth. **toll**

11. It _____to be seen whether his company will be a success or not. **remains**

12. He is wondering when the update on the project will be _____ . **finished / completed / done / underway / finalized**

13. The IT company is designing a special computer _____ for some new clients. **program / programme / system / application / app**

14. He mentioned that he is going to need some _____ to get the job done on time. **help / assistance**

15. I'll _____ you an email to let you know how it's going. **send**

16. The prisoner _____ from jail, but was caught two days later. **escaped**

17. He was born in India, but his family _____ to the United States when he was a little boy. **moved / emigrated**

18. She's really talented and can _____ some beautiful music on the piano. **play**

Test 3 Part E – Dictation

1. They asked us to work this weekend.

2. There were a lot of people there, and it was quite crowded.

3. We have had to raise prices to cover our costs.

4. She's going to return to work tomorrow.

5. The company is experiencing financial problems.

6. His assistant handles all of his travel arrangements.

7. She says she really likes working there.

8. He said he was going to have to work late.

9. The people in this town seem really nice.

10. The job offers a better position with more pay.

11. Due to unforeseen circumstances, today's meeting has been canceled.

12. She always puts her phone in the pocket inside her coat.

13. I'll contact you next week to firm up the plans.

14. She was hoping for some rest and relaxation.

Test 3 Part F – Passage Reconstruction (Sample responses)

A pipe had sprung a leak under Marta's sink, so she had to call in a plumber to repair it. She paid the plumber for his work, and he left. But then she noticed that the pipe continued to leak, so she called the plumber and asked him to come back. He refused to come back and said he had already finished the job. Marta thought the plumber was really unprofessional, so she reported the incident to the mayor.

Alice took her bike for a ride in the park in the city on a nice, sunny summer day. The birds were singing, and Marta was having a good time, but then there was a strange noise, and the bike began to move in an unusual way. She realized that the tire was flat once she had gotten off of the bike. She knew she couldn't ride it anymore, so she walked home with it that way.

Versant 4-Skills Practice Test 4 – Answers

Test 4 Part A – Repeat

1. We've made special arrangements for the additional number of customers.

2. With all the programs available, it can be hard to know which to choose.

3. I emailed the document to him yesterday.

4. This office is such a mess.

5. Sorry, but I'm running a bit late.

6. The volume of the speaker wasn't loud enough.

7. I'm sorry, but that item is out of stock.

8. Everyone tried to act like nothing had happened.

9. Check in at the reception desk before you sit down.

10. Over the last twenty years, this company has changed a lot.

11. The electrician said that he would call tomorrow with the estimate.

12. Have you taken a break yet?

13. Sorry, I must have dialed the wrong number.

14. Where is the exit nearest to the office?

15. The technology sector is growing in this country.

16. You will need to speak to the director about that.

Test 4 Part B – Sentence Builds

1. staying here / how long / is he

   Answer: How long is he staying here?

2. of her house / some pictures / she has

   Answer: She has some pictures of her house.

3. these mistakes / corrected / need to be

   Answer: These mistakes need to be corrected.

4. across the street / for sale / is the house

   Answer: Is the house across the street for sale?

5. the bus / in thirty minutes / should arrive

   Answer: The bus should arrive in thirty minutes.

6. is more important / experience / than training

   Answer: Experience is more important than training.

7. your name / on this form / be sure you sign

   Answer: Be sure you sign your name on this form.

8. to learn / he is trying / English

   Answer: He is trying to learn English.

Test 4 Part C – Conversations

Conversation 1:
Are you done reading this book?
I'm not reading it. You can take it if you want to.
Thanks! I'll return it next week.
What did the woman borrow?
Answer: the man's book

Conversation 2:
I'm going for a walk later.
You should take an umbrella in case it rains
Thanks for reminding me.
What will the man take on his walk?
Answer: an umbrella

Conversation 3:
Is the train the quickest way to get to your house?
Actually, I think the bus is faster. The train has a lot of delays.
Thanks for letting me know.
How will the man travel to the woman's house?
Answer: the bus

Conversation 4:
According to the weather forecast, it's going to snow tomorrow.
Maybe we can go skiing this weekend.
We'll have to remember to take along everything we need.
What are they hoping to do this weekend?
Answer: go skiing

Conversation 5:
Did you tell the boss that you were sick yesterday?
Yes, I told him this morning.
I only asked because we're supposed to do it.
What happened to the man yesterday?
Answer: He was sick.

Conversation 6:
John is such a friendly person.
I know. I really like him too.
I'm going to see him tomorrow.
Why do they like John?
Answer: because he is a friendly person

Conversation 7:
Are you going to see your friends on Sunday?
No, I need to work some extra hours.
Maybe you can see them next Sunday.
What will the man do this weekend?
Answer: work some extra hours

Conversation 8:
The manager didn't come to the meeting yesterday.
Why not?
I guess he had a last-minute emergency.
Who didn't attend the meeting yesterday?
Answer: the manager

Conversation 9:
When I got there, she wasn't even at home.
So, what did you do?
I just came back here.
What happened to the woman?
Answer: Her friend wasn't at home.

Conversation 10:
My mother is really a great cook.
I think she's the best cook in the world.
Me too.
What did the man say about his mother?
Answer: She is a great cook.

Conversation 11:
Do you want to eat at that new restaurant tonight?
I don't really feel like it.
Okay, maybe some other evening.
What does the woman suggest?
Answer: eating at the new restaurant

Conversation 12:
Are you still working in the call center?
Yes, I really like it.
It must be a good job.
Where is the man working?
Answer: in the call center

Test 4 Part D – Sentence Completion

1. What do you _____ for a living? **do**

2. How much does this book _____? There's no price on it. **cost**

3. My _____ is very large. There are my parents and twelve siblings. **family**

4. She can _____ five different languages fluently. **speak**

5. There were many guests at the celebration, so it was a bit _____ inside. **crowded**

6. An increasing _____ of families are experiencing financial problems. **number** (Note: "amount" is incorrect because "families" is a countable noun.)

7. I don't _____ what he wrote to me. I'm going to tear up that letter and throw it away. **like**

8. The game had to be _____ indefinitely because of the damage to the stadium. **postponed** (Note that "cancelled" is incorrect because of the word "indefinitely.")

9. He asked the politician a bunch of questions that she didn't have time to _____ . **answer / address**

10. My boss complimented me yesterday by _____ how efficient I am. **saying / mentioning**

11. He was really feeling depressed. The bad news really got him _____ . **down**

12. The supermarket has many different _____ of fruit and vegetables. **kinds / types / varieties**

13. Littering is _____ the law, and if you do so, you will have to pay a fine. **against**

14. You can't smoke in here. In fact, smoking is _____ in the entire building. **prohibited / forbidden**

15. He seemed very rude. He didn't _____ "hello" or greet us in any way. **say**

16. My parents have _____ me a great deal of support throughout my life. **given**

17. You shouldn't swim too _____ out in the sea because of the dangerous tides. **far**

18. She had to hurry to work today to avoid _____ late. **being**

Test 4 Part E – Dictation

1. I'm afraid I disagree with you.

2. At the moment, it's raining really heavily.

3. We should be able to find a way forward if we put our heads together.

4. She said she really enjoyed her meal.

5. Customers should note that our phone number and email will remain the same.

6. The train arrived half an hour late.

7. I'm looking forward to seeing you tomorrow.

8. Having a hobby is good for your mental health.

9. The store is always so busy, especially on the weekends.

10. I need to work until 9:00 o'clock tonight.

11. Would you consider moving if we offered you a transfer?

12. Many people dream of getting a well-paid office job.

13. Please have the report ready by the weekend.

14. Profits were much higher than the company had expected.

Test 4 Part F – Passage Reconstruction (Sample responses)

The company wanted to tell everyone to plan for the company picnic on the 11th of June, which is a Saturday. There is going to be a band called Infinity, and there will also be a barbeque. Employees were told to bring along friends and family members.

The company advised all of its employees that gym membership would no longer be offered for free. The gym's fees had doubled in price because its costs had gone up. So, now the employees can carry on with their gym membership for half of the new price. To do this, they need to get in touch with Brooke in HR.

Versant 4-Skills Practice Test 5 – Answers

Test 5 Part A – Repeat

1. Which jacket is yours?

2. Exit through the door on your left.

3. She wanted to know whether the price included meals.

4. You need final written approval for the project.

5. Management reserves the right to refuse service to anyone.

6. I nearly missed the train this morning.

7. How are we going to be able to fit all of this on one page?

8. Many people feel nervous before speaking in front of a group.

9. His flight leaves for London at 10:30 PM.

10. The authors of this book wanted to add more drawings.

11. Orders placed over the telephone must be collected at customer service.

12. The reason for that policy was never clear to me.

13. Please bring two reference letters with you to the interview.

14. Would you be willing to take a cut in pay to learn a new job?

15. The pay raise was too low for me to continue working there.

16. Would you please send me the package as soon as possible?

Test 5 Part B – Sentence Builds

1. looking forward / they were / to the new office

   Answer: They were looking forward to the new office.

2. on Saturday / to see his brother / he left

   Answer: He left on Saturday to see his brother. / On Saturday, he left to see his brother.

3. cleaned up / needs to be / that mess

   Answer: That mess needs to be cleaned up.

4. the report / deleted / she accidentally

   Answer: She accidentally deleted the report.

5. screen each visitor / the security guard / needs to

   Answer: The security guard needs to screen each visitor.

6. a recent article / in detail / described the problems

   Answer: A recent article described the problems in detail.

7. good results / is expected to show / the report

   Answer: The report is expected to show good results.

8. about that / has a policy / the company

   Answer: The company has a policy about that.

Test 5 Part C – Conversations

Conversation 1:
I'm sorry, but I can't let you in.
But I have my employee pass, and I come here a lot.
Yes, but it's expired.
Why can't the woman come in?
Answer: Her pass is expired.

Conversation 2:
Where can I get more information about that new job?
The company website tells you everything you need to know about it.
Great! Thanks for your help.
What information is on the company's website?
Answer: information about the new job

Conversation 3:
I arrived at work twenty minutes late yesterday.
You'd better be careful about that.
I know. You're right.
Why does the man need to be careful?
Answer: because he arrives at work late

Conversation 4:
I don't know what I feel like eating tonight.
Maybe you'll know later.
I think you're probably right.
What is the woman talking about?
Answer: She doesn't know what to eat tonight.

Conversation 5:
The company I work for is going to close down.
So, what are you going to do now?
I don't know yet.
What problem does the man have?
Answer: His company is closing down.

Conversation 6:
Did he say to turn right at the corner?
I didn't hear him.
Well, let's try it.
What was the woman asking about?
Answer: getting directions / whether to turn right at the corner

Conversation 7:
Are you enjoying being married?
Yes, I'm really happy.
I'm so glad to hear that.
Why is the man so happy?
Answer: He is enjoying being married.

Conversation 8:
I think she has three children, doesn't she?
Yes, all of them are at college.
They must be clever.
How many of their friend's children are at college?
Answer: three

Conversation 9:
Next week, the company is going to receive an award.
What for?
Because they have a great customer service record.
What is happening to the company next week?
Answer: It will receive an award.

Conversation 10:
I couldn't understand the instructions for the copy machine.
Me either.
We will have to ask someone who knows how to use it.
What couldn't the man and woman understand?
Answer: the instructions for the copy machine

Conversation 11:
I'm hoping to travel to America next year.
What cities will you go to?
I'm not sure.
What is the woman hoping to do next year?
Answer: travel to America

Conversation 12:
The city has a big problem with litter.
I know. I went there last week.
I think they need to do something about it.
What problem does the city have?
Answer: There is a big problem with litter.

Test 5 Part D – Sentence Completion

1. I woke up late but arrived on _____ at the conference. **time**

2. You will need to show your passport or some other form of _____. **identification**

3. The tasks were _____ among all the team members. **divided / split**

4. The building had only been finished for a month when the _____ sold it. **owner**

5. Plastic bottles can be _____ and used to make things like clothing and packaging. **recycled**

6. Customers will receive a 5% _____ for ordering and paying online. **discount**

7. The movie star made an _____ at the film premiere. **appearance**

8. He was trying to get on the boss's _____ side by giving her compliments. **good**

9. I'm having second _____ about my plan and regret agreeing to do it. **thoughts**

10. Please get in touch _____ me next week so we can talk. **with**

11. We have _____ preparing the meal, so please sit at the table. **been / finished**

12. I apologize. I meant to _____ you about the party last week. **tell**

13. I'm really tired of _____ to him complain all the time. **listening**

14. The movie wasn't _____. I left half-way through. **interesting / funny / good**

15. The company is split into two departments. The security department is _____ new, but the computing department is much older. **quite / rather**

16. If you would like to know what my daughter looks like, have a _____ at these pictures. **look**

17. His brother, _____ name is Samuel, is studying to become a lawyer. **whose**

18. She was fired for cheating _____ her pre-employment test. **on**

Test 5 Part E – Dictation

1. There's going to be a party for all of the employees.

2. I don't like eating a big dinner.

3. Where is the paper that we use in the copy machine?

4. His house is so nice and comfortable.

5. The flight will depart in two hours.

6. It's too cold out, so we'd better stay in today.

7. The agreement needs to be signed in front of two other people.

8. The company will need two references for you.

9. I can't think of a better solution right now.

10. She likes dogs as well as cats.

11. There will be extra charges for paying late.

12. He really can't stand going to the cinema.

13. If you need some help, just let me know.

14. The house was cleaned inside and out.

Test 5 Part F – Passage Reconstruction (Sample responses)

Neal answers customer calls in a call center that is always busy. A customer called one day and was very upset because his new computer wouldn't work. Neal told the customer that the company would either repair the computer or give the customer a refund. The customer decided to get his money back, so the call went well in the end.

Debbie and Karl had a new nephew that they were going to see for the very first time. They were so eager to meet him and bought him some gifts, including a new shirt and a toy dinosaur. When they gave their nephew the gifts, he was really pleased and happy. He wore his new shirt right away and enjoyed playing with the dinosaur.

Versant 4-Skills Practice Test 6 – Answers

Test 6 Part A – Repeat

1. Operating expenses for the quarter were less than budgeted.

2. Call centers are springing up all over this area.

3. I know I won't be able to get away before 6:30.

4. Everyone knows they made a large profit on that deal.

5. She reminded me to send the invoice two weeks ago.

6. After July 31, our service charges will have to be increased.

7. We offer discounts for companies that make larger purchases.

8. Late charges will be added to your bill after the 15th.

9. Surprisingly, Carmen managed to get enough money together for her trip.

10. The repair project is going to cost five thousand dollars altogether.

11. What time do you usually wake up in the morning?

12. I'd like to have one too.

13. The letter needs to get there by Thursday.

14. Take some time to think about the situation before you respond.

15. Refusing to follow the dress code can result in suspension and loss of pay.

16. Stealing from the company is grounds for immediate dismissal.

Test 6 Part B – Sentence Builds

1. until next Monday / staying here / is she

   Answer: Is she staying here until next Monday?

2. he is / now / leaving

   Answer: He is leaving now.

3. outside today / very hot / it is

    Answer: It is very hot outside today.

4. all of / were clean / the windows

    Answer: All of the windows were clean.

5. sign in / are expected to / all employees

    Answer: All employees are expected to sign in.

6. than expected / lasted longer / our meeting

    Answer: Our meeting lasted longer than expected.

7. than small ones / earn more money / big projects

    Answer: Big projects earn more money than small ones.

8. orders must / before 12 o'clock / be placed

    Answer: Orders must be placed before 12 o'clock.

Test 6 Part C – Conversations

Conversation 1:
I need to pay for my parking.
I thought parking on Main Street was free.
Yes, but only on Saturday and Sunday.
Where is the man parked?
Answer: on Main Street

Conversation 2:
I'm going to have to change my plans for the party.
What happened?
I need to go out of town this weekend.
What does the woman need to change?
Answer: her plans for the party

Conversation 3:
I finished writing that big report on Thursday.
You must feel relieved.
Of course. I really do.
What did the man finish on Thursday?
Answer: writing that big report / that big report

Conversation 4:
They should deliver the new furniture on Friday.
I've heard that they're having delays.
I heard that too. We'll see.
What should be done on Friday?
Answer: The new furniture should be delivered.

Conversation 5:
The door is broken.
Have you reported it?
Good idea. I'll do it now.
What problem did the man mention?
Answer: the broken door / that the door is broken

Conversation 6:
Where's the nearest copy machine?
There's one next to the back door.
Okay. Thanks.
What is located next to the back door?
Answer: the nearest copy machine

Conversation 7:
Are you living in Los Angeles?
No, I'm from Las Vegas.
I've heard it's really exciting to live there.
Where does the woman live?
Answer: Las Vegas

Conversation 8:
Would you like to come to the museum with me?
I can't. I'm helping my mother.
Okay. Maybe next weekend.
Why can't the man go to the museum?
Answer: He's helping his mother.

Conversation 9:
I feel like eating at that new restaurant tonight.
I've heard it's expensive.
So do you want to come?
What did the man think was expensive?
Answer: eating at that new restaurant / the new restaurant

Conversation 10:
Do you do any hobbies in your free time?
Yes, I love reading technical magazines.
That sounds interesting.
What does the man do in his free time?
Answer: reading technical magazines

Conversation 11:
Tomorrow, let's meet by that beautiful flower garden.
Okay. What time shall we meet?
Around 2 o'clock.
Where will they meet tomorrow?
Answer: by the flower garden / by that beautiful flower garden

Conversation 12:
Can I bring something along for our picnic?
You could bring something to drink.
Okay. I'll do that.
What will the woman bring to the picnic?
Answer: something to drink

Test 6 Part D – Sentence Completion

1. It was really _____ outside and no one wanted to leave the warm house. **cold**

2. I don't have my phone. I must have _____ it at the restaurant. **left / forgotten**

3. It looks like this final _____ of the letter is ready to go out. **version / draft**

4. Remember to _____ for her phone number when meet her. **ask**

5. I lost my _____ because I was shouting at the game yesterday. **voice**

6. I was given office supplies, consisting _____ paper and pens. **of**

87

7. She said she had _____ to do with the missing money. **nothing**

8. If you don't know the _____ to the question, just guess. **answer / response**

9. Some people like the opera, but I can't _____ it. **stand**

10. I don't like getting coffee in the mall, so I'd _____ go to that cafe in town. **rather**

11. He was speaking so softly that we couldn't _____ what he was saying. **hear / understand**

12. I am enjoying my new job now that I have gotten used _____ it. **to**

13. He gets the _____ grades of all the students in his class. **best / highest**

14. In _____ to jogging, Susan also likes to ride her bike. **addition**

15. The weather report said that people should _____ for bad weather. **prepare**

16. Sarah _____ everyone my secret, but I forgave her. **told**

17. He would have bought that new car if he'd had more _____. **money**

18. She finally decided to _____ college after she got a scholarship. **attend**

Test 6 Part E – Dictation

1. The leak in the sink has just been repaired.

2. Please be sure to check the spelling and grammar on all of your reports.

3. They presented a proposal to expand the company.

4. Why aren't you eating anything?

5. I was afraid something was going to go wrong.

6. If you need any help, just give me a call.

7. I threw those old newspapers away.

8. Please report to my office at 9:00 AM.

9. The deadline for the project is next Friday.

10. There shouldn't be any delay in getting the job done.

11. If only we didn't have to work this weekend!

12. It would be a good idea to put in some extra effort.

13. I can't find a copy of that report anywhere.

14. The company announced that there were going to be some cut backs.

15. I don't exercise as often as I should.

16. Please be sure that all of the checks and controls have been carried out.

17. Our new boss is really treating us like a team.

18. He said he was going to arrive twenty minutes late.

Test 6 Part F – Passage Reconstruction (Sample responses)

Employees were being thanked for attending a class on security online on the weekend. There were classes in password security and spam. The employees who participated were going to get a certificate of attendance for the classes.

Kay and Mark had their 25th anniversary over the weekend and wanted to celebrate it. They were going to spend the night in a hotel and go out for a meal out. They drove into the city in their car and were looking forward to having a romantic evening. But when they got to the hotel, they were told that they hadn't reserved a room. So, they spent the night in a more expensive hotel instead.

Versant 4-Skills Practice Test 7 – Answers

Test 7 Part A – Repeat

1. I think I'll have one as well.

2. Take a little time to think about the options available.

3. Where is the ink cartridge for the printer?

4. You don't like my ideas, but can you suggest something better?

5. The delivery arrived yesterday at 5:00 PM.

6. I'd like to take three vacation days next week.

7. She'll be working from home for the rest of the week.

8. I'm going to need help to finish this on time.

9. Here is my email address and phone number.

10. That was on my desk, so can you please put it back?

11. She needed to read the documents before attending the meeting.

12. He just started work last week.

13. She has ten people reporting to her now.

14. Can you give me the status of your progress so far?

15. Please give me a draft by the end of next week.

16. He said that it was sent by registered mail.

Test 7 Part B – Sentence Builds

1. remember to / workspace tidy / keep your

   Answer: Remember to keep your workspace tidy.

2. by the 31st / are due / all payments

   Answer: All payments are due by the 31st.

3. a website / should have / every business

    Answer: Every business should have a website.

4. you should / for a job interview / always prepare

    Answer: You should always prepare for a job interview.

5. five years ago / started nearly / the company

    Answer: The company started nearly five years ago.

6. considered to be / she was / a valuable employee

    Answer: She was considered to be a valuable employee.

7. bright colors / don't like / some people

    Answer: Some people don't like bright colors.

8. paid immediately / need to be / the charges

    Answer: The charges need to be paid immediately.

Test 7 Part C – Conversations

Conversation 1:
What are you reading right now?
A really interesting history book.
That does sound really interesting.
What kind of book is the woman reading?
Answer: a really interesting history book / a history book

Conversation 2:
That new cafe is offering coffee for free this week.
I saw that in the paper.
Maybe we should go there for lunch.
What is special about the new cafe?
Answer: It is offering free coffee.

Conversation 3:
How was your holiday?
Great. I really enjoyed the beach.
That sounds really relaxing.
What did the man enjoy?
Answer: the beach / his holiday

Conversation 4:
It's really quiet in the library.
They have rules about that.
Oh, of course.
What did the man say about the library?
Answer: It is really quiet.

Conversation 5:
When are you going to see your parents?
I hope to see them this weekend.
I hope you have a good time.
What is the woman hoping to do this weekend?
Answer: see her parents

Conversation 6:
You need to print those documents.
Okay, how do I do it?
No problem. I'll show you.
What is the man going to show the woman?
Answer: how to print the documents

Conversation 7:
Do you want to go for a walk with me?
I just finished one.
Where did you go?
What did the man just finish?
Answer: a walk / going for a walk

Conversation 8:
Can I borrow your chair?
Yes, when I'm finished writing this email.
Thanks. I'll wait.
What item does the man want to borrow?
Answer: the woman's chair

Conversation 9:
Did you see the recent email to everyone?
Yes, it said they may hire some new employees.
I hope so.
What communication have the speakers received about new employees?
Answer: an email

Conversation 10:
Our chances of getting a raise are good.
I hope so.
Yes, me too.
What do the man and woman hope will happen?
Answer: that they will get a raise

Conversation 11:
What do you think about this new policy?
I'm not sure I understand it.
I'm a little confused about it too.
What are the speakers confused about?
Answer: the new policy

Conversation 12:
Any news about our new boss?
They said she'll arrive next month.
That will be great.
What are the two people speaking about?
Answer: their new boss / the arrival of their new boss

Test 7 Part D – Sentence Completion

1. Ted enjoys singing, as _____ as dancing. **well**

2. You're walking too _____ . Please slow down. **fast / quickly**

3. I slept too long this morning and was _____ for work. **late**

4. To _____ for that job, you need to have a degree from a college or university. **apply / qualify**

5. I need to _____ the post office of my new address. **inform**

6. I told him I would pick him _____ this morning in my car. **up**

7. I _____ to his house last weekend. **went / traveled**

8. Could you please _____ the window to let in some fresh air? **open**

9. I thought I had lost my keys, but I managed to _____ them later. **find**

10. Let's keep seeing each other every month. I would hate it if we lost _____ with each other. **touch / contact**

11. He _____ his English placement exam, but hopes to pass it the next time. **failed / flunked**

12. All of the employees were gathered around the table to discuss the project at the team _____ . **meeting**

13. He had a nice job and a good income, but then he got _____ off. **laid**

14. We need to _____ this invoice by the end of the week to avoid the late fee. **pay / clear / cover**

15. If you are not in support of the plan, then you must be _____ it. **against**

16. The company policy says that all employees need to _____ a uniform. **wear**

17. The result _____ the discussion was that the company decided to hire more staff. **of**

18. You will need to show respect _____ your boss to succeed at work. **for**

Test 7 Part E – Dictation

1. If you aren't going to come, please let us know.

2. He takes the train to work every day.

3. The company is controlling spending to increase its profits.

4. It's a nice day for a walk in the park.

5. They failed to reach an agreement on the new proposal.

6. Companies are often understaffed these days.

7. They told us they would be cutting down our hours.

8. The event is going to take place in the city park.

9. We're going to have to inform the customers about the change.

10. The manager will return to the office at 4:00 o'clock.

11. The company had to close its San Francisco office.

12. If you'd like an appointment, please have a word with my assistant.

13. Do you like living here?

14. She said she was hoping to finish work early.

15. The restaurants here are so expensive.

16. I accepted the job because it meant I'd earn more money.

17. We are going to have to hold the meeting a little earlier today than planned.

18. The document is on my desk next to the phone.

Test 7 Part F – Passage Reconstruction

Martin is an 85-year-old man who lives in a retirement community in his town. He is happy for the most part, even though he misses his children sometimes when they can't come to visit him. He dines with the other people who live there, and he likes the food. He also thinks that the nurses who work there are very attentive and good at their jobs.

Bart was really looking forward to taking a vacation in Costa Rica. He was an adventure lover, so he was going to water ski and mountain climb there. Then he had an accident on his motorcycle the day before he was going to leave, and he couldn't go. So now he is hoping to be able to go next year.

Versant 4-Skills Practice Test 8 – Answers

Test 8 Part A – Repeat

1. She used to be one of my co-workers.

2. I think I'll take the day off tomorrow.

3. He has ten years' experience in this line of work.

4. Please analyze all of the data completely for your review.

5. Do you have the weekly report on the integration project?

6. He is going to be busy every single day next week.

7. She'll be available to take our call only after 2:30 PM.

8. I'm afraid I won't be able to read it until the weekend.

9. Can you come right over to my office?

10. He worked an hour late yesterday, so he'll arrive an hour later today.

11. Your sick days cannot be carried forward to next year.

12. She wanted to know whether she could do it later.

13. I consider him to be very reliable.

14. She has never let us down before now.

15. What is the deadline for this report?

16. You can reach me by calling the phone number at the bottom of my email.

Test 8 Part B – Sentence Builds

1. her name / know / I don't

   Answer: I don't know her name.

2. Friday off / is taking / she

   Answer: She is taking Friday off.

3. increase prices / needed to / the company

   Answer: The company needed to increase prices.

4. be given / bonuses will / for excellent performance

   Answer: Bonuses will be given for excellent performance.

5. than before / many more customers / the company has

   Answer: The company has many more customers than before.

6. July is / for vacation / a popular month

   Answer: July is a popular month for vacation.

7. she regretted / her boss / shouting at

   Answer: She regretted shouting at her boss.

8. more supplies / to purchase / we need

   Answer: We need to purchase more supplies.

Test 8 Part C – Conversations

Conversation 1:
I'm getting a new computer on Wednesday.
Oh! That's great!
Yes, I can't wait.
What will the woman receive on Wednesday?
Answer: a new computer

Conversation 2:
Is your son on the football team?
Yes, he has just been chosen as the captain.
How wonderful!
What sport does the man's son play?
Answer: football

Conversation 3:
I need to work really hard to prepare for this interview.
You should read the information about the company.
I've already done that.
What is the woman preparing for?
Answer: a job interview

Conversation 4:
The boss didn't say much at the meeting.
I was surprised about that too.
I know. She was really quiet.
Why are the man and the woman surprised?
Answer: The boss didn't say much at the meeting. / The boss was quiet at the meeting.

Conversation 5:
I just got a funny email from my sister.
What did she say?
I don't think I should repeat it.
What did the woman get from her sister?
Answer: a funny email

Conversation 6:
Please log on with your username and password.
How do I do that?
The system will show you how.
What does the woman need to do?
Answer: log on / log on to the computer

Conversation 7:
How is that project going?
Terrible. I've had a lot of problems.
Sorry to hear that.
What is the man having problems with?
Answer: his project / a project

Conversation 8:
Do you think it's going to rain?
Probably. It looks cloudy.
I thought so too.
What do the speakers think is going to happen?
Answer: that it will rain / that it is going to rain

Conversation 9:
I finally got promoted to manager.
That's great.
Well, I hope I like it.
What has happened to the woman?
Answer: She got promoted to manager. / She got promoted.

Conversation 10:
Are you going to come to our house on Sunday?
I'm afraid I can't.
What happened?
What is the woman unable to do?
Answer: go to the man's house on Sunday

Conversation 11:
This food tastes like it's spoiled.
It must have been left out of the refrigerator.
We shouldn't eat it.
What's wrong with the food?
Answer: It is spoiled. / It has been left out of the refrigerator.

Conversation 12:
What kind of work will we have to do next week?
The boss said we'll continue filing reports.
I feel so bored with that.
What job makes the woman feel bored?
Answer: filing reports

Test 8 Part D – Sentence Completion

1. It is _____ outside today, so I don't think I'll need a sweater. **hot / warm**

2. She works really slowly, so I _____ that she'll finish the job on time. **doubt**

3. The man was shouting and screaming, but people took no _____ of him. **notice**

4. The company policy has _____ recently regarding time off. **changed**

5. Could I have a smaller _____ of cake please? **piece / slice / portion / serving**

6. Will you please turn _____ the TV? I'd like to watch it. **on**

99

7. My bus was delayed in traffic, so I _____ late. **was / arrived**

8. If you make a _____, then you should clean it up yourself. **mess**

9. I hope to go on _____ to California next year. **vacation / holiday**

10. They didn't have the item, but they said it would be _____ next week. **available**

11. I would prefer to speak to someone in _____, rather than over the phone. **person**

12. We need to _____ all staff that the store will be closed next week. **inform / tell**

13. I need a _____ cable because this one is too long. **shorter**

14. The document was placed in the wrong mail box _____ mistake. **by**

15. I am completely fed up _____ this terrible situation. **with**

16. The store doesn't accept credit cards. You will need to pay in _____. **cash**

17. It is so noisy in the next room. We should tell them to be _____ . **quiet**

18. I don't think you will get away _____ leaving work early every day. **with**

Test 8 Part E – Dictation

1. All of the employees of this company are team members.

2. Customers can always send items back to us to get a refund.

3. I just can't agree with you about this.

4. If we work together, we'll be able to find a good solution.

5. He mentioned that his brother lives in Chicago.

6. The contact information for our new boss is provided in the email.

7. There was an accident, and the road was closed.

8. I wanted to arrive early to get everything ready.

9. Being lonely can have a negative effect on your health.

10. The store is offering large discounts to attract new customers.

11. I've had to work late every night this week.

12. Would you consider working more hours if we offered you a promotion?

13. Some people can't stand the thought of sitting at a desk all day long.

14. She told him that his performance had been disappointing.

Test 8 Part F – Passage Reconstruction (Sample responses)

Frankie was hoping to get a new car, and she had been shopping around for one for several weeks. She had seen ads and had also talked to some salespeople. She found one on the internet that she thought was just right for her, so she decided to buy it. It was a little red car with a powerful engine that would be really good for driving in the traffic.

George wanted to try something new at his job, so he filed an application for a job teaching company employees how to use their computer system. Up to that point, he had been in the computer department working on online security. He found the security job kind of boring because he didn't get to interact with any of his co-workers. But he got the new job, meets new people every day, and is really enjoying it.

Versant 4-Skills Practice Test 9 – Answers

Test 9 Part A – Repeat

1. Do you know any good places to eat near here?

2. There's a bank right across the street from the office.

3. He left his laptop at a friend's house.

4. I need to know what you're planning to do next week.

5. What's the status of the marketing program?

6. I'm afraid I can't hear you very well.

7. I'll be sure that she gets your message today.

8. He was pleased to receive our response to his proposal.

9. The report indicates trends in the business sector.

10. Twenty years ago, informality in business was not acceptable.

11. All employees are kindly requested to refrain from smoking.

12. There's no point in trying to add more information.

13. Important topics should never be mentioned after the close of a meeting.

14. The president decided not to attend the conference.

15. Their products are always of very high quality.

16. All of these articles need to be inspected before shipment.

Test 9 Part B – Sentence Builds

1. I'm sorry / hear you / I can't

    Answer: I'm sorry I can't hear you.

2. of hers / a co-worker / he is

    Answer: He is a co-worker of hers.

3. him again / to see / I was so surprised

   Answer: I was so surprised to see him again.

4. my big brother / than me / is taller

   Answer: My big brother is taller than me.

5. the flight / two hours / was delayed

   Answer: The flight was delayed two hours.

6. report is / overdue / that financial

   Answer: That financial report is overdue.

7. sales started / in January / to decline

   Answer: Sales started to decline in January.

8. she is / person / a very kind

   Answer: She is a very kind person.

Test 9 Part C – Conversations

Conversation 1:
My boss was in a car accident.
That's terrible.
I know. I don't know how it happened.
What happened to the man's boss?
Answer: He was in a car accident.

Conversation 2:
My dad really likes to bake cake.
I know. I had some last month.
I love it too.
What does the woman's father enjoy doing?
Answer: baking cake / to bake cake

Conversation 3:
Is the plane the best way to get to Chicago?
Actually, I think the train is better.
Okay. I'll try that instead.
According to the man, what is the best way to travel to Chicago?
Answer: the train / by train

Conversation 4:
Will we be paid back for our expenses?
I really don't know.
Maybe we should ask someone.
What are the speakers talking about?
Answer: payment for their expenses / whether they will be paid back for their expenses

Conversation 5:
Do you want to go out this weekend?
No, I don't really feel like it.
Okay, maybe another time.
What does the man suggest?
Answer: going out this weekend / going out another time

Conversation 6:
It's supposed to be really hot this weekend.
Maybe we can go to the beach.
That would be great.
How is the weather going to be this weekend?
Answer: really hot

Conversation 7:
Didn't you say that you lost your phone?
Yes, I'll have to buy a new one.
I hope it's not too expensive.
What happened to the woman?
Answer: She lost her phone.

Conversation 8:
Are you using this chair?
No, I'm not. You can take it if you want to.
Thanks so much.
What did the man want to use?
Answer: the chair / the woman's chair

Conversation 9:
I'm going out for lunch.
Can I come?
You'd be most welcome.
Where are the speakers going?
Answer: out for lunch

Conversation 10:
My son is getting quite tall.
So he'll be like your husband.
I think you're right.
What's happening to the woman's son?
Answer: He is getting quite tall.

Conversation 11:
Are you going to have to clean your house today?
No, I'll put it off until next weekend.
That's probably a good idea.
What will the man put off until next weekend?
Answer: cleaning his house

Conversation 12:
Are you still working as a sales assistant?
Yes, but I'm looking for something else.
So you don't like it.
What kind of work is the man doing?
Answer: He is a sales assistant.

Test 9 Part D – Sentence Completion

1. He is far _____ stupid. In fact, he is the most intelligent person I know.
   from

2. This coat is really _____. I would like a cheaper one. **expensive / costly / dear / pricey**

3. That restaurant is really busy, so you will need to make a _____ if you want to eat there. **reservation**

4. She was sitting _____ them, with Cindy on her left and Ian on her right. **between**

5. The lecture was so dull that I thought I was going to fall _____ . **asleep**

105

6. I often have _____ with getting to sleep at night, especially when I'm worried about something. **trouble / problems / difficulty / difficulties**

7. He never quite got _____ their argument and continues to be upset about it. **over**

8. He wanted to lose weight and decided to _____ more. **exercise**

9. My watch is broken. Could you tell me the _____ please? **time**

10. If you are _____, you should have something to eat. **hungry**

11. Entering the museum is _____ . You don't need to pay anything. **free**

12. My grandma is coming to visit me _____ the beginning of the month. **at**

13. If she is asking you too many questions, tell her to mind her own _____ . **business**

14. They disagree with the plan, and they are going to _____ to it at the next meeting. **object**

15. How is everything _____ for you with your new job? **going**

16. The manager needs to sign the document to show that she _____ of it. **approves**

17. What you have requested is impossible. I mean, it's really out of the _____. **question**

18. She had a bad accident, but the doctor said she will pull _____ and recover from her injuries. **through**

Test 9 Part E – Dictation

1. He wasn't able to finish the project on time.

2. The ticket is in the pocket of my coat.

3. We're going to be informed about the change in policy next week.

4. You can use this work station once I'm finished.

5. He doesn't really like going out at night.

6. The company report indicated a huge drop in profits.

7. She likes to go swimming, especially in the summer.

8. The information on the new jobs will be published on the company's website.

9. I really wasn't sure if we were doing the right thing.

10. He thought that it was too late to make any changes.

11. The company is going to improve the quality of the product.

12. I would love some cake with my coffee.

13. She wasn't able to arrive on time.

14. The workload was demanding, and the pay was low.

Test 9 Part F – Passage Reconstruction (Sample responses)

Ray and Nancy's young son was invited to a children's costume party. All of the kids were going to wear different costumes, so it was bound to be fun. They went shopping for the costume with their boy, and he chose a pirate's outfit. He liked the costume so much, and he particularly loved the pirate's hat that was included with the costume.

Rosa's much-loved hobby is growing flowers in her garden in her backyard. She waters and cares for the plants every morning. Sometimes she even takes cut flowers from the garden to make a flower arrangement for her house. In her opinion, gardening is one of the best pastimes.

Versant 4-Skills Practice Test 10 – Answers

Test 10 Part A – Repeat

1. You can't access that computer software right now.

2. The development manager needs to allow enough room for new employees.

3. Computers should be turned off at the end of the day.

4. The report should have been spell checked.

5. He spent hours editing that document before he sent it.

6. I see from your resume that you were a manager in your last job.

7. Can you please tell us something about your plans for the future?

8. We sometimes have to deal with disappointed or angry customers.

9. He was fired because he always handed his work in late.

10. There is a large difference between the money needed and the money available.

11. When you retire, you may be eligible for a pension.

12. People put money into a business in the hope of making a profit.

13. In the end, we will need to earn some money from the investment.

14. There is still an outstanding balance on that account.

15. This failure is a good example of what not to do.

16. Plans are already in place to deal with the situation.

Test 10 Part B – Sentence Builds

1. in my opinion / too much money / it isn't

    Answer: In my opinion, it isn't too much money. / It isn't too much money in my opinion.

2. the expenses / than expected / were less

    Answer: The expenses were less than expected.

3. special equipment / a piece of / that is

    Answer: That is a piece of special equipment.

4. the maintenance cost / to decrease / is going

    Answer: The maintenance cost is going to decrease.

5. for three hours / went down yesterday / the system

    Answer: The system went down for three hours yesterday. / For three hours, the system went down yesterday.

6. our network providers / one of / they are

    Answer: They are one of our network providers.

7. be reduced / email needs to / the volume of

    Answer: The volume of email needs to be reduced.

8. approval must / in advance / be given

    Answer: Approval must be given in advance.

Test 10 Part C – Conversations

Conversation 1:
My sister is going to travel to Australia in September.
How exciting.
I know. I'm really happy for her.
What's the man's sister going to do in September?
Answer: travel to Australia

Conversation 2:
That town has three new apartment buildings.
That's quite a lot.
I know. That doesn't happen very often.
What's happening in the town?
Answer: It has three new apartment buildings.

Conversation 3:
You need to provide your password before we can continue.
I was told never to share that.
Yes, you need to change it after we've spoken.
What does the woman need to provide?
Answer: her password

Conversation 4:
Who should I send my job application to?
You can send it to the HR Department.
Okay. Thanks for the information.
What will the man send to the HR department?
Answer: his job application

Conversation 5:
I'm going to move to Sydney.
How exciting. When are you leaving?
At the end of the month.
What will the woman do at the end of the month?
Answer: move to Sydney

Conversation 6:
That company has to pay some fines.
What happened?
I'm not really sure.
What does the company need to do?
Answer: pay some fines

Conversation 7:
The department I work in has three new jobs available.
Why did that happen?
I don't really know.
What is happening in the man's department?
Answer: It has three new jobs available. / There are three new jobs available.

Conversation 8:
Did he say to go straight along this road?
I think so.
Okay. Let's go.
What direction will they travel on the road?
Answer: straight / straight ahead

Conversation 9:
Are you enjoying your new baby?
Yes, I'm just thrilled.
I'm so glad.
What is the man enjoying?
Answer: his new baby

Conversation 10:
I need to go to work early tomorrow.
What time?
Before 7:30 in the morning.
What does the woman need to do tomorrow?
Answer: go to work early / go to work before 7:30

Conversation 11:
Have you read the instructions for the new computer system?
Not yet.
Me either.
What haven't the speakers read?
Answer: the instructions for the new computer system

Conversation 12:
I would really rather stay at home tonight.
Are you tired?
Yes. I really am.
What does the man want to do tonight?
Answer: stay at home

Test 10 Part D – Sentence Completion

1. If you are out alone at night, you need to look _____ for danger. **out**

2. My parents _____ each other for the first time when they were at college. **met**

3. She is a lot of _____ because she is always telling jokes. **fun**

4. If you _____ more money than you have, you might get into debt. **spend**

5. The economy is going to _____ from the serious recession last year. **recover**

6. I don't need that anymore. You can _____ it away. **throw**

111

7. The weather was bad, so we _____ our picnic until next week. **postponed**

8. I am in a hurry, so I don't have _____ to talk now. **time**

9. The new machinery was expensive, but the cost seems to have been _____ it so far. **worth**

10. She was really happy _____ getting the big promotion. **about**

11. There has been a mix up. I need to _____ things right. **get / put / make**

12. If you hadn't eaten so much, you wouldn't have gotten a _____ ache. **stomach**

13. You're a fool if you believe her because she has _____ us many lies. **told**

14. I didn't _____ on seeing him. Running into him was a coincidence. **plan / count**

15. I have no _____ where your book is. It could be anywhere. **idea**

16. He is unwell. In fact, he's been feeling _____ the weather for a few days. **under**

17. The report showed better results than anyone _____. **expected**

18. Many people feel shy about _____ in a foreign language. **speaking**

Test 10 Part E – Dictation

1. There's going to be a party to celebrate his retirement.

2. He really enjoys eating at that new restaurant.

3. Where is the ink that we use in the printer?

4. Her house is a bit small, but it has a big garage.

5. We're going to have to change our plans completely.

6. Some people love to go skiing when it's snowy outside.

7. The buyer didn't sign the agreement, so the sale didn't go through.

8. It's a good idea to keep your resume up to date.

9. I think it would be better if we did nothing.

10. He really enjoys playing online computer games.

11. There is a 10-day grace period before payment is considered late.

12. She's going to go see that new movie on the weekend.

13. I needed help, but no one was around to assist me.

14. We need to keep this workspace clean and organized.

Test 10 Part F – Passage Reconstruction

Sample responses:

Darleen had lived in the city for ten years when she decided to move to the country. She was eager to move into her big country house, and hoped to get some animals, like a cat, dog, or horse. When Darleen moved into the big country house, she didn't enjoy living there because she felt isolated and alone. Finally, she made the decision to move back into the city.

Tony prepares documents for a lawyer, and he is always busy. He has access to an advanced computer network where he can see all of the legal information he needs for his job. One day he was in the middle of a big project, when the system crashed. Tony's boss was irate when the project wasn't ready. Tony then told him about the problem with the computer system, and he apologized.

Made in the USA
Las Vegas, NV
05 August 2024

93394626R00070